P9-DGD-937

The (Very Latest)

Vermont Quiz Book

The (Very Latest)
Vermont Quiz Book

Compiled and Edited
by
Melissa Lee Bryan
Frank Bryan

Photographs by Linda Bryan

The New England Press, Inc.
Shelburne, Vermont

© 2002 by Melissa Lee Bryan and Frank Bryan

All rights reserved. No part of this book may be reproduced or transmitted in any form or by any means, electronic or mechanical, including photocopying, recording, or by any information storage and retrieval system, without permission in writing from the publisher.

First Edition
Book Design by Mark Wanner
Production and Cover Design by Christopher A. Bray
Library of Congress Catalog Card Number: 2001095994
ISBN 1-881535-42-8
Printed in the United States of America
06 05 04 03 02   5 4 3 2 1

Also by Frank Bryan (with Bill Mares):
The Vermont Owner's Manual
Out! The Vermont Secession Book
Out of Order! The Very Unofficial Vermont State House Archives

For additional copies or a catalog of our other titles, please write:

The New England Press
P.O. Box 575
Shelburne, Vermont 05482

or e-mail: nep@together.net

Visit us on the Web at www.nepress.com

For Rachel and Frank,
good kids

Contents

Introduction

The original *Vermont Quiz Book* was published in 1986. It enjoyed a successful run, and despite multiple printings, every copy printed had sold out by 1990. We all wanted to print more so we could sell more, but time had moved along, and too many questions were, well, old. (A favorite is a photograph of George Bush, Sr., with Jim Jeffords that asks "What is the vice president saying to the congressman?") It was clear that the book needed a major revision before we could send it to the stores again.

Updating the entire book proved a daunting task, so years came and went without a new *Quiz Book*. But we couldn't leave it alone (actually, our publisher wouldn't let us), and so at the beginning of the new century, faced with a vastly different Vermont than the one we quizzed so thoroughly fifteen years ago, we are doing it again. There are questions here that didn't change at all—the foundation of Vermont's character is its history, after all—but many are brand new. In 1986, after all, "civil union" probably would have been used in reference to a harmonious multi-town school district.

As before, we have tried to add a human touch to this book—values and motivation. We seek to share the passion of Robert Rogers, the wisdom of George Aiken, the true Yankee wit. With photographer Linda Bryan's help, we hope to show glimpses of Vermont's many sides—the beauty of the Connecticut River Valley near Newbury in summer, and Essex Junction's traffic-clogged Five Corners in the rain.

Furthermore, we wanted this book to be educational as well as fun. Don't panic. We are both teachers, and we both believe education can be fun. It's fun to know, and it's fun to be (mildly) competitive about learning. Someone once said that the true mark of educated people is that they know how much they don't know. After crafting, assessing, and checking nearly 1,000 questions about Vermont, we have come to realize how much there is to know, really know, about the Green Mountain State. If we've been at all success-ful with this book, then you should have the same reaction we did—"Whew . . . I didn't realize there was so much to know!"

John Dewey, himself a Vermonter, once observed that the total educational experience for an entire year of a child's schooling ought to be focused on one thing, a grand focal point from which all learn-ing—math, history, art, whatever—would be drawn. Not a bad idea. Could there be a better theme than Vermont? We don't think so, and we hope *The (Very Latest) Vermont Quiz Book* helps you on your own journey of discovery of this unique and superb little state.

Acknowledgments

In addition to the many people who were part of the first edition (especially Jeff Olson), we wish to thank our friends and neighbors (too numerous to mention) who made suggestions for the current edition. Special help was provided by Stephanie and Genie O'Neil (our Internet specialists), Rebecca Cole, Bill Mares, many staff members of the UVM library, and the helpful folks in agencies of Vermont state and local government. Thank goodness too for the patient and professional work of Mark Wanner, who edited this edition, and Christopher Bray, also of The New England Press, who put on the finishing touches. Finally, as always, we want to pay special tribute to Maggie and Al Rosa of The New England Press, whose enthusiasm and faith make it so much fun to write (and learn) about Vermont.

Melissa and Frank Bryan

October, 2001

CHAPTER 1

Old Ruggedness, New Softness*

Vermont Geography

Perhaps one reason why Vermont is so unique is that the linkage between people and place—its geography—is so clear. Vermont is a land of ups and downs, hills and dales, nooks and crannies. Its hundreds of rivers and streams have cut and rounded (and even flattened here and there) places for us to live. Before the bulldozer was discovered that was how it, blessedly, had to be. Whereas before we put our houses where the land was right, now we put the land where we want our houses. And sooner or later we'll pay for it!

1. The highest village in the state, at 2,215 feet above sea level, is
   a. Woodbury.
   b. Woodford.
   c. Woodstock.
   d. Adamant.

2. The area from Springfield to Ludlow was known as Vermont's
   a. Precision Valley.
   b. Champlain Valley.
   c. Hoosic Valley.
   d. Winooski Valley.

*Charles W. Johnson describes Vermont in his *Nature of Vermont* as follows: "Vermont is modestly grand, a softness over old ruggedness, blessed with diversity of land and wildlife."

3. How big is the Northeast Kingdom?

   a. 600 square miles
   b. 2,000 square miles
   c. 5,000 square miles
   d. 10,000 square miles

4. Interstate 89 extends all the way from New Hampshire to Canada. The highest point on this highway is

   a. north of Sharon, south of Montpelier.
   b. south of Sharon.
   c. north of Montpelier, south of St. Albans.
   d. north of St. Albans.

5. You are driving south on I-89 and you have just passed the exit for Sharon. The next large river you cross is the

   a. Black River.
   b. White River.
   c. Connecticut River.
   d. Winooski River.

6. Three rivers—the Passumpsic, Moose, and Sleepers—meet in what town?

7. Montpelier was named for a small city in

   a. New York.
   b. Moldavia.
   c. France.
   d. England.

8. How long is Vermont?

   a. About 100 miles
   b. About 150 miles
   c. About 250 miles
   d. About 300 miles

9. Of the following, which town is the northernmost?
   a. Morgan
   b. St. Albans
   c. Newport
   d. Lowell

10. Of the following, which is the southernmost?
    a. Vernon
    b. Brattleboro
    c. Bennington
    d. Wilmington

11. Which town does not border on the Connecticut River?
    a. Hartland
    b. Westminster
    c. Guildhall
    d. Groton

12. Pick out the two towns in Bennington County.
    a. Readsboro
    b. Jamaica
    c. Charleston
    d. Arlington

13. Interstate 91 does not pass through one of these. Which one?
    a. Barton
    b. Newbury
    c. Putney
    d. Windham

14. The top of Vermont runs along which parallel?
    a. 55th
    b. 50th
    c. 45th
    d. 40th

On the map below locate the following and place the correct letter by the number of the question:

15. _____ Mt. Philo
16. _____ Camel's Hump
17. _____ Rutland City
18. _____ Pittsford Ice Caves
19. _____ Burke Mountain
20. _____ The West River
21. _____ Mount Equinox

22. _____ Chazgan Coral Reef
23. _____ Devil's Gulch
24. _____ The Batten Kill River
25. _____ George Aiken's Hometown
26. _____ Appalachian Gap
27. _____ Hogback Ski Area
28. _____ Vermont Marble Exhibit

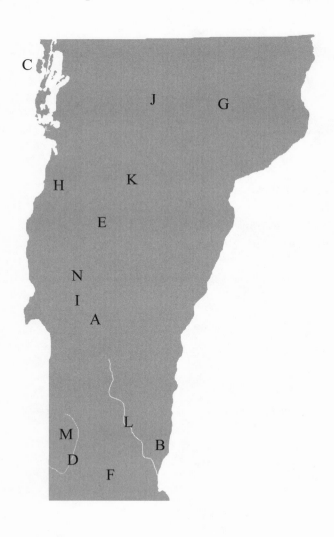

29. The Connecticut River belongs to

    a. Connecticut.
    b. New Hampshire.
    c. Vermont.
    d. Vermont and New Hampshire jointly.

30. If you were to walk around the entire shoreline of Lake Champlain, you would

    a. walk over 500 miles.
    b. be walking around the largest fresh water lake in the U.S. excluding the Great Lakes.
    c. both a and b.
    d. neither a nor b.

31. What does the Indian name for Champlain, "Petonbowk," mean?

    a. Lake of Shining Waters
    b. Waters Long and Blue
    c. Waters that Lie Between
    d. Lake of the Abenaki Nation

32. Just below the source of the West River along Route 100 and surrounded by the Green Mountains, you will find the village of

    a. Weston.
    b. Newfane.
    c. Plymouth.
    d. Ludlow.

33. The state capital is on what river?

34. Which is the biggest lake completely within the state's border?

    a. Bomoseen
    b. Seymour
    c. Carmi
    d. Harriman Reservoir (also called Lake Whitingham)

35. Which town is closest to the center of the state?

    a. Ludlow
    b. Randolph
    c. Moretown
    d. Stockbridge

36. In which direction does Lake Champlain flow?

37. Ticklenaked Pond is in the town of

    a. Groton.
    b. Ryegate.
    c. Clarendon.
    d. Newport.

38. Which one is not a "gore"?

    a. Avery
    b. Warren
    c. Buels
    d. Lewis

39. In what town did the Runaway Pond run away?

40. What's another name for the "Onion River"?

41. According to the state tourism Web site, the "Crossroads of Vermont" usually refers to the intersection of

    a. Route 4 and Route 7.
    b. Route 2 and Route 100.
    c. Route 11 and Route 100.

42. Which lake is *not* in the Northeast Kingdom?

    a. Lake Salem
    b. Lake Seymour
    c. Echo Lake
    d. Lake Bomoseen

Match the river with the body of water it flows into.

River | | *Body of Water*
43. _____ The Batten Kill | | a. Lake Memphremagog
44. _____ The Clyde | | b. Lake Champlain
45. _____ The Lamoille | | c. The Connecticut River
46. _____ The Saxtons | | d. The Hudson River

47. In the town of Newbury the Connecticut River forms great shapes in the land that have been named the big and the little _____.

48. One of Vermont's lakes has an Indian name that means "Beautiful Waters." It is

   a. Ninevah.
   b. Winnipesaukee.
   c. Memphremagog.
   d. Willoughby.

Match the town on the left with the one on the right that borders it to the east:

49. _____ Rupert | | a. Guilford
50. _____ Sheffield | | b. Fairfax
51. _____ Georgia | | c. Sutton
52. _____ Halifax | | d. Dorset

53. Pensioner Pond, Lubber Lake, Lake Salem, and Lake Memphremagog are all connected by the

   a. Clyde River.
   b. Barton River.
   c. Nulhegan River.
   d. Connecticut River.

54. What do the following towns and cities have in common?

   Guildhall, Burlington, Hyde Park, Newfane, Chelsea

55. Lake Morey is a popular summer getaway in which part of the state?
  a. Eastern
  b. Western
  c. Southern
  d. Northern

56. There are actually 4 rivers in the White River system. The main branch, however, begins in which town?

  a. Washington
  b. Roxbury
  c. Ripton
  d. Williamstown

57. The source of the Ompompanoosuc River is in the town of

  a. Mount Holly.
  b. Dorset.
  c. Greensboro.
  d. Vershire.

58. What is the *Horse Ferry?*

  a. Another name for the UVM Horse Farm
  b. A Lake Champlain underwater historic site for scuba divers
  c. The last horse-drawn ferry across the Clyde in Newport
  d. The original name of the Grand Isle ferry

59. Which mountain is within twenty miles of the Massachusetts border?

  a. Mount Anthony
  b. Seneca Mountain
  c. Roosevelt Mountain
  d. Mount Tabor

Answers
Vermont Geography

1. b. Woodford.
2. a. Precision Valley. It was the center of the machine tool industry in the 19th and 20th centuries.
3. b. 2,000 square miles
4. a. north of Sharon, south of Montpelier.
5. b. White River.
6. St. Johnsbury
7. c. France.
8. b. 157.5 miles to be exact.
9. c. Newport
10. a. Vernon
11. d. Groton
12. a. and d. Readsboro and Arlington
13. d. Windham
14. c. 45th parallel
15. H Mt. Philo
16. K Camel's Hump
17. A Rutland City
18. N Pittsford Ice Caves
19. G Burke Mountain
20. L The West River
21. M Mount Equinox
22. C Chazgan Coral Reef
23. J Devil's Gulch
24. D The Batten Kill River
25. B George Aiken's Hometown (Putney)
26. E Appalachian Gap
27. F Hogback Ski Area
28. I Vermont Marble Exhibit
29. b. New Hampshire.
30. c. both a and b.
31. c. Waters that Lie Between
32. a. Weston
33. The Winooski River

34. d. Harriman Reservoir with 2,496 acres. If you answered Bomoseen with 2,395 acres, call it close enough. (Carmi in Franklin has 1,417 acres and Seymour in Morgan has 1,723 acres.)
35. b. Randolph
36. North
37. b. Ryegate.
38. d. Lewis
39. Glover
40. The Winooski River
41. a. Route 4 and Route 7 in Rutland.
42. d. Lake Bomoseen
43. d. The Hudson River
44. a. Lake Memphremagog
45. b. Lake Champlain
46. c. The Connecticut River
47. oxbows
48. c. Memphremagog. (Of course you knew that Winnipesaukee is in New Hampshire!)
49. d. Rupert—Dorset
50. c. Sheffield—Sutton
51. b. Georgia—Fairfax
52. a. Halifax—Guilford
53. a. Clyde River.
54. They are all the shire towns of their county.
55. a. Eastern
56. c. Ripton
57. d. Vershire.
58. b. One of several underwater historic sites for scuba divers in Lake Champlain
59. a. Mount Anthony (near Bennington)

CHAPTER 2

Nice States Finish First

Is it pride or is it self-defense when Vermonters bristle up and proclaim: "But did you know Vermont is the first state that . . .?" One can imagine the flatlander's inner thoughts: "In New York we have so many firsts we lost count in 1832." Anyway, for a state with a population about the size of Syracuse, New York, we think Vermont does pretty well. Besides, if what our publishers tell us is true, Vermont is the only state in the union to have a decent (60.) _____ _____ book written exclusively for it!

61. Vermont was the first state to join the Union after the original thirteen.

   a. True
   b. False

62. The nation's first ski tow was located in

   a. Killington.
   b. Stowe.
   c. Woodstock.
   d. Burke.

63. The first canal in the country was built in 1802 in

   a. Bellows Falls.
   b. White River Junction.
   c. Isle La Motte.
   d. Winooski.

64. The first female lieutenant governor ever elected in the United States was elected in Vermont.

    a. True
    b. False

65. The first shot fired in the War of 1812 was fired in Vermont.
    a. True
    b. False

66. Norwich University, the nation's first private military school, was originally established in _____ and later moved to _____.

    a. Northfield, Norwich
    b. Newbury, Northfield
    c. Putney, Norwich
    d. Norwich, Northfield

67. The Dresdan School District was the first school district in the U.S. to unite towns on opposite sides of a state boundary. The towns are

    a. Stamford, Vermont and Willliamstown, Massachusetts.
    b. Lunenburg, Vermont and Lancaster, New Hampshire.
    c. Alburg, Vermont and Rouses Point, New York.
    d. Norwich, Vermont and Hanover, New Hampshire.

68. The first normal school in America was founded in _____, Vermont, in 1823.

    a. Newbury
    b. Wilmington
    c. Fletcher
    d. Concord

69. The American flag, featuring the "stars and stripes," was first used in battle in Vermont.

    a. True
    b. False

70. The first American patent, signed by George Washington, was issued in 1790 to a Vermonter for

a. potash.
b. an apple cider press.
c. chewing tobacco.
d. ox yokes.

71. The first (and longest) alpine slide in North America is at what ski area?

a. Stowe
b. Killington
c. Bromley
d. Ascutney

72. "Snowflake" Bentley of Jericho was the first person to photograph snowflakes. Snowflake's first name was really

a. Calvin.
b. William.
c. Hiram.
d. Wilson.

73. Vermont was the first state to allow women to vote.

a. True
b. False

74. Vermont was the first state to adopt universal manhood suffrage.

a. True
b. False

75. The nation's first chairlift was used in 1940 on

a. Madonna Mountain.
b. Okemo Mountain.
c. Mount Mansfield.
d. Mount Ascutney.

76. A Vermonter was the first person ever to cross the United States by automobile.

    a. True
    b. False

77. The nation's first marble quarry was started at

    a. East Dorset by Isaac Underhill.
    b. Proctor by Redfield Proctor.
    c. Isle La Motte by Henry Ripley.
    d. East Barre by John Judd.

78. Scottish immigrant William F. Milne organized the first _____ in 1909 while living in Barre.

    a. educational society
    b. Boy Scout Club
    c. museum
    d. labor union

79. In the Revolutionary War, Solomon Brown of New Haven, Vermont, was the first to

    a. enlist in the Continental Army.
    b. shoot a British soldier.
    c. enlist in the American Navy.
    d. die in the Battle of Bunker Hill.

80. Senator Warren Austin of Burlington, Vermont, was America's first

    a. Ambassador to the Soviet Union.
    b. senator to denounce McCarthyism.
    c. Ambassador to the United Nations.
    d. senator to vote to declare war on Japan.

81. Vermont's constitution was the first to abolish the requirement that voters must be property owners.

    a. True
    b. False

82. On one particular January 31ˢᵗ, Ida M. Fuller of Ludlow received $22.54. On that day she became America's first

    a. lottery winner.
    b. recipient of Social Security.
    c. woman to earn money as a politician.
    d. beneficiary of a life insurance policy.

83. The first _____ _____ (two words) used in America was made in Brattleboro in 1846.

84. The nation's first school of higher education for women was established in

    a. Bennington.
    b. Burlington.
    c. Middlebury.
    d. Rutland.

85. Vermont's constitution was the first state constitution to outlaw slavery.

    a. True
    b. False

86. It was in Vermont that the first African American

    a. received a college degree.
    b. became a state legislator.
    c. received an honorary college degree.
    d. all of the above.

87. The first international railroad junction in the United States—connecting Portland, Maine, with Montreal, Quebec—linked the Canadian National Railway with the Atlantic & St. Lawrence Railroad in the Vermont town of

    a. Derby.
    b. Newport.
    c. Orleans.
    d. Island Pond.

88. In 1896 Vermont passed the first law that would allow you to carry your politics with you. What was it?

89. Which of the following is a federal program first used in Vermont?
    a. Head Start
    b. Civilian Conservation Corps
    c. CETA
    d. FDIC

90. What "Vermont First in the Nation" happened on July 1, 2000?

91. Which of the following is *not* a Vermont first?
    a. The first tri-town water district in the nation
    b. The first death caused by a snowmobile accident in the nation
    c. The first woman admitted to practice law before the Supreme Court
    d. The first French-Catholic parish in America

92. Vermont was the first state to create a state publicity service to promote tourism.
    a. True
    b. False

93. Vermont was the first state in which a commercial pet cemetery was established.
    a. True
    b. False

94. The first comedy to be professionally staged in America was written by a man who lived in Vermont.
    a. True
    b. False

95. Vermont was the first state to award baccalaureate and graduate degrees in agriculture.

   a. True
   b. False

96. In 1985 a college in Putney opened as the country's first college specifically for

   a. fiddle music and contra dancing.
   b. paralyzed students.
   c. equestrian studies.
   d. dyslexic students.

97. Henry Cushman of Bennington is credited with having been the first to use the

   a. rubber eraser.
   b. time clock.
   c. stopwatch.
   d. ballpoint pen.

98. In 1971 Vermont became the first state in the nation to bestow full adult responsibilities and privileges on eighteen-year-olds.

   a. True
   b. False

99. The first known spy to defect to the Soviet Union after World War II was a Vermonter from the village of Moscow.

   a. True
   b. False

100. The first air traffic regulation course was offered in Vermont.

   a. True
   b. False

101. Vermont was the first state to do all of the following *except*

    a. issue the first seeding-machine patent.
    b. adopt anti-sit-down strike legislation.
    c. have the first steam-heated factory.
    d. use automatic milking-machines on cows.

102. Vermont was the first state in the U.S. to swear in an all-woman jury.

    a. True
    b. False

103. Vermont was the first state to have a state symphony orchestra.

    a. True
    b. False

104. Vermont was the first state to outlaw capital punishment.

    a. True
    b. False

Answers
Nice States Finish First

60. quiz
61. a. True
62. c. Woodstock.
63. a. Bellows Falls.
64. a. True. Consuelo N. Bailey was elected in 1954.
65. b. False
66. d. Norwich, Northfield. Established in 1819, it offered the first civil engineering course.
67. d. Norwich and Hanover.
68. d. Concord
69. a. True
70. a. potash. It's a granular substance created from wood ashes and used in making soap. It was first made by Samuel Hopkins, but controversy now surrounds this patent. Some facts indicate it was issued to another Samuel Hopkins, who hailed from Philadelphia.
71. c. Bromley Ski Area
72. d. Wilson.
73. b. False
74. a. True
75. c. Mount Mansfield.
76. a. True. Burlington physician H. Nelson Jackson started out from San Francisco in 1903.
77. a. East Dorset by Isaac Underhill in 1785.
78. b. Boy Scout Club
79. b. shoot a British soldier.
80. c. Ambassador to the United Nations.
81. a. True
82. b. Ms. Fuller received check number 00-000-001 in 1940 for Social Security benefits.
83. postage stamp
84. c. Middlebury (established in 1814 by Emma Willard).

85. a. True
86. d. all of the above.
87. d. Island Pond.
88. An absentee voting law
89. a. Head Start (started in East Fairfield)
90. Act 91 went into effect granting same sex civil unions.
91. b. The first death caused by a snowmobile accident
92. a. True. The first advertisement used to promote Vermont was entitled: "Vermont, Designed by the Creator for the Playground of the Continent."
93. b. False
94. a. True. Royall Tyler wrote *The Contrast* in 1787. Today the Royall Tyler Theater at the University of Vermont offers a variety of theatrical entertainment.
95. b. False (It was Pennsylvania.)
96. d. dyslexic students (Landmark College).
97. a. rubber eraser.
98. b. False
99. b. Sure, and the Pope's Italian.
100. a. True, at Norwich University in 1934.
101. d. use automatic milking-machines on cows.
    The first seeding-machine patent went to Eliakim Spooner in 1799; Vermont enacted anti-sit-down strike legislation in 1937; the Burlington Woolen Company was the first steam-heated factory in 1846.
102. b. Nope (Wyoming has that claim to fame.)
103. a. True
104. b. False

THE VERMONT
INVENTORS' PAGES

105. David Smith of Springfield is credited with inventing the

    a. combination lock.

    b. computer mouse.

    c. post-it note.

    d. mop wringer.

Match the inventor with the invention or discovery for which he is known:

_____	106. Benjamin J. Wheeler Calais, 1868	a. Steel carpenter's square
_____	107. Thomas Davenport Brandon, 1837	b. Globe
_____	108. Thaddeus Fairbanks St. Johnsbury, 1830	c. Electric motor
_____	109. Silas Hawes Shaftsbury, 1817	d. Platform scale
_____	110. James Wilson Bradford, 1810	e. Carriage brakes

111. The nation's first marble-cutting saw was invented in 1837 by

    a. Thaddeus Grant of Proctor.

    b. Hiram Kimball of Stockbridge.

    c. Henry Bennett of Barre.

    d. William Parkington of Bellows Falls.

112. Vermont inventors John Cooper and Asahel Hubbard came up with the first

    a. turret lathe.

    b. windshield wipers.

    c. spoon fishing lure.

    d. rotary pump.

113. Joel A. Ellis of Springfield has been credited as the inventor of American

    a. toy carts.
    b. violin cases.
    c. jointed dolls.
    d. all of the above.

114. Fourteen years before Fulton ran the *Clermont* up the Hudson, Vermonter Samuel Morey ran a paddlewheel steamboat on the Connecticut River.

    a. True
    b. False

115. John M. Weeks of Salisbury invented

    a. the first beehive that didn't kill the bees when honey was taken.
    b. the first egg "grader" that separates white from brown eggs.
    c. the first automated gutter cleaner for dairy barns.
    d. the bunker silo.

116. Gardner Springs Blodgett designed the first

    a. microwave oven.
    b. cast iron cooking oven.
    c. pizza oven.
    d. crock pot.

117. One of the ships in the famous battle between the *Monitor* and the *Merrimack* was built by a Vermonter. Which ship?

118. One of the most famous Green Mountain Boys was an inventor. One of his inventions was a corn-crusher. Who was he?

    a. Ethan Allen
    b. Remember Baker
    c. Seth Warner
    d. Peleg Sunderland

119. Sandpaper was invented in Vermont.

    a. True
    b. False

120. Gardner Colton of Georgia, Vermont, was the first to discover

    a. maple sugar.
    b. seltzer water.
    c. laughing gas.
    d. phosphate fertilizer.

121. Duncan Holaday of Barnet created a unique use for milk by using it in the making of

    a. teeth whitener.
    b. maple syrup.
    c. vodka.
    d. bleach.

122. Robert Sysling, a Jericho resident, recently received a patent for

    a. heated windshield wipers.
    b. wireless inkjet printers.
    c. chicken manure fuel.
    d. a maple syrup purifying machine.

Answers
Inventors' Pages

105. a. combination lock (also the first adding machine, corn planter, and breech-loading rifle).
106. e. Benjamin Wheeler invented effective carriage brake systems.
107. c. Thomas Davenport invented the electric motor. (He also invented the first electric piano and electric printing press.)
108. d. Thaddeus Fairbanks invented the platform scale. (He also invented the first iron plow and refrigeration method.)
109. a. Silas Hawes invented the steel carpenter's square.
110. b. James Wilson invented the first American globe. (He later established a globe factory.)
111. b. Hiram Kimball of Stockbridge.
112. d. The rotary pump, which they invented in the early 1800s. The turret lathe was invented by a Springfield man, James Hartness, in 1891; windshield wipers were actually invented by a woman from Alabama; and the spoon fishing lure was created by Julio Buel of Castleton.
113. d. all of the above.
114. a. True (Morey's steamboat operated in 1793.)
115. a. John M. Weeks invented a beehive that allowed you to extract the honey without killing the bees. He wasn't a real Vermonter since he was born in Connecticut and lived a full year there before coming to Vermont in 1789.
116. b. In 1848 he came up with a cast iron wood-burning oven.
117. John F. Winslow built the Union's *Monitor* (the ship that won). He was born in Bennington in 1810.
118. b. Remember Baker
119. a. True, in 1834 by a Springfield man, Isaac Fisher, Jr.
120. c. laughing gas. Then Horace Wells used it as an anesthetic for pulling teeth in 1844.
121. c. vodka. He uses lactose to make Vermont Spirits White Vodka.
122. a. heated windshield wipers.

CHAPTER 3

Natural Vermont

When Sam Hand and Nick Muller decided to publish an edition of articles on Vermont history, they entitled it *In a State of Nature*. Good choice. For when one hears the world Vermont, one thinks "natural": one thinks hillsides and ponds and bogs and pastures and forests. And one thinks of the living creatures that crawl, slither, fly, swim, run, flutter, flit, and float above and below, in and among, and roundabout this incredibly beautiful state of ours. Living in Vermont unconscious of the natural world would be like living in Washington unconscious of politics. Or living in Arizona unconscious of the sun. This section judges your capacity to accept Vermont's greatest gift, the chance to live with nature.

123. About how many moose were in Vermont in 2000?

    a. 3,000
    b. 5,000
    c. 7,000
    d. 10,000

124. Becoming a menace to lake trout and other large fish in Lake Champlain are

    a. leeches.
    b. Champ.
    c. sea lampreys.
    d. otters.

125. Two troublesome species that have disrupted the ecology of Lake Champlain in recent times are the zebra mussel and the _____ _____.

126. Between 1959 and 1967 Vermont imported 124 _____
from Maine to help reduce the damage caused by porcu-
pines.

   a. fisher cats
   b. weasels
   c. bobcats
   d. coyotes

Vermont is a tough land. We take our pleasures where we find
them. One of those pleasures is the birds that sing and swoop or
sometimes just sit there and look, well, pretty. Or interesting.
Or awesome. See if you can match the bird with the peculiar
characteristic attributed to it.

   a.   Eastern Phoebe
   b.   Cowbird
   c.   House Wren
   d.   Killdeer

_____ 127.   Leaves its eggs in other birds' nests and lets them
              do the upbringing.
_____ 128.   Sometimes punctures an opponent's eggs with its
              bill.
_____ 129.   Builds its nest on the ground, not in a tree.
_____ 130.   Sees an insect fly by, darts out, catches it, and
              twitches its tail when perched.

131. You can get arrested these days for being too interested in
exotic *grass* found in out-of-the-way places in Vermont.
Of the following, which is a real wild grass found in Vermont?

   a. Mohawk Grass
   b. Barnyard Grass
   c. Maple Grass
   d. Goldenrod

132. Which one usually attains a greater weight at maturity, a
snapping turtle or a river otter?

133. One of the most frightening sounds one can hear in the woods of Vermont is the scream of a bobcat. In which month are you most likely to hear it?

    a. June
    b. September
    c. January
    d. March

To live happily in Vermont it is essential to know the language—especially those items of the natural world known by popular terms. Here is a list of names you may hear in Vermont. What do they stand for? Some answers may be used more than once.

		Answers
___ 134.	Shepherd's Purse	a. A bird
___ 135.	Woolly Bear	b. A wildflower
___ 136.	Stinking Benjamin	c. A caterpillar
___ 137.	Lady Slipper	d. A turtle
___ 138.	Bobolink	e. A frog
___ 139.	Fiddlehead	f. A fish
___ 140.	Stinkpot	g. A duck
___ 141.	Dutchman's Breeches	h. A butterfly
___ 142.	Peeper	i. A fern
___ 143.	Northern Leopard	
___ 144.	Pumpkin Seed	
___ 145.	"Bog Bull"	
___ 146.	Mourning Cloak	
___ 147.	Maidenhair Spleenwort	
___ 148.	Bullhead	

149. "Timberdoodle" is another name for a

    a. mushroom.
    b. woodpecker.
    c. woodcock.
    d. logger.

150. Wildflowers are a sure sign of spring and, like the coming of the songbirds, are the object of such happy cries as "Guess what I saw today!" One of the following is a rare and beautiful wildflower of Vermont that blooms closer to autumn than spring and, like the early twilight, signals the coming of winter.

    a. Lady slipper
    b. Trailing arbutus
    c. Fringed gentian
    d. Hepatica

151. Vermont is less forested now than it was 100 years ago.

    a. True
    b. False

152. Vermont can be divided into six biophysical regions: Green Mountains, Northeast Highlands, Piedmont, Champlain Valley, Taconic Mountains, and

    a. Upland Plateau.
    b. Valley of Vermont.
    c. Lower Canadian Plain.
    d. Appalachian Trail.

153. One gender of the mallard duck does not quack. Is it the male or the female?

154. Scientists in Addison County have recently discovered an endangered species visiting and reproducing in Vermont. Look out for

    a. Indiana Bats.
    b. Prairie Chickens.
    c. Orange-bellied Parakeets.
    d. Black-footed Ferrets.

155. Vermont has no poisonous rattlesnakes.

    a. True
    b. False

156. One of Vermont's most important naturalists began his public career with a magazine article on the subject of fox hunting in New England. He also published sketches for *Forest and Stream* that reappeared in his book *Uncle Lisha's Shop*. He did most of his writing while blind. He was from Ferrisburg and died in 1900.

His name was Rowland Evans _____.

Throughout its history, Vermont has had many books written about its natural quality. Can you match the author(s) with the book?

_____157. Charles Johnson   a. *Natural History of Vermont*

_____158. Zadock Thompson   b. *The Story of Vermont: A Natural and Cultural History*

_____159. George Aiken   c. *Vermont's Land and Resources*

_____160. Christopher Klyza and Stephen Trombulak   d. *The Nature of Vermont*

_____161. Harold A. Meeks   e. *Pioneering with Wildflowers*

162. The top twig of a hemlock tree always points

    a. east.
    b. west.
    c. north.
    d. south.

163. Name the wildflower that is also called dragonroot, starch plant, and memory root. Hints: Think church. The roots are edible if cooked or dried out. _____

164. Perhaps Vermont's most popular modern nature writer, author of *Loon in My Bathtub, How Do You Spank a Porcupine?, Animals Nobody Loves,* and other books, was

_____.

165. Goldeneyes, ringnecks, lesser scaup, and buffleheads are the most common

    a. wild turkeys.
    b. squirrels.
    c. diving ducks.
    d. rabbits.

166. What do these names have in common?

    Peacham
    Molly
    Franklin
    Chickering

167. Vermont's world-renowned conservationist of a century ago was George Perkins _____.

Anyone living in Vermont for the last thirty years or so is aware of the balance between change and permanence. Some things seem to endure forever. Others seem to melt away, slowly and unnoticed. Some things we try to protect. Others we do not. Below is a list of things found in Vermont. Place them in the proper category of *"endangerment."*

	These are on the official Vermont Endangered Species List	These are not on the official Vermont Endangered Species List	These are not on the official Vermont Endangered Species List but should be!
168. Eastern Mountain Lion	_____	_____	_____
169. Dutch Elm	_____	_____	_____
170. Chittenden County	_____	_____	_____
171. Barn Swallow	_____	_____	_____
172. Common Tern	_____	_____	_____
173. Lake Sturgeon	_____	_____	_____

	These are on the official Vermont Endangered Species List	These are not on the official Vermont Endangered Species List	These are not on the official Vermont Endangered Species List but should be!
174. Great Blue Heron	_____	_____	_____
175. Fisher Cat	_____	_____	_____
176. Republicans	_____	_____	_____
177. American Moose	_____	_____	_____
178. Lady Slipper	_____	_____	_____
179. Spruce Grouse	_____	_____	_____
180. Common Loon	_____	_____	_____
181. Town Meeting	_____	_____	_____
182. Bald Eagle	_____	_____	_____
183. Timber Rattlesnake	_____	_____	_____
184. Bearberry Willow	_____	_____	_____
185. Raven	_____	_____	_____
186. Lynx	_____	_____	_____
187. Skidway Header	_____	_____	_____
188. Coydog	_____	_____	_____
189. Spotted Turtle	_____	_____	_____
190. The Real Vermonter	_____	_____	_____

31

191. This 40-mile-long lake actually lies mostly in Quebec. You can hop on board the *Stardust Princess* for a delightful sightseeing cruise on

    a. Island Pond.
    b. Lake Memphremagog.
    c. Crystal Lake.
    d. Echo Lake.

192. Nestled between Mt. Hor and Mt. Pisgah, this lake is also known as the "Lucerne of America."

    a. Lake Willoughby
    b. Caspian Lake
    c. Lake Seymour
    d. Lake Champlain

Answers
Natural Vermont

123. a. 3,000
124. c. sea lampreys.
125. water chestnut
126. a. fisher cats
127. b. Cowbird
128. c. House Wren
129. d. Killdeer
130. a. Eastern Phoebe
131. b. Barnyard Grass
132. A snapping turtle can grow to 3 feet long and weigh 50 pounds while a river otter is usually 25 pounds.
133. d. March, which is their mating season.
134. b. Shepherd's Purse is a spring wildflower.
135. c. Woolly Bear is a caterpillar.
136. b. Stinking Benjamin is a wildflower.
137. b. Lady Slipper is a wildflower.
138. a. Bobolink is a blackbird.
139. i. Fiddlehead is a fern.
140. d. Stinkpot is a turtle.
141. b. Dutchman's Breeches is a wildflower.
142. e. Peeper is a tiny frog.
143. e. Northern Leopard is a frog.
144. f. Pumpkin Seed is a fish.
145. a. "Bog Bull" is one of the nicknames for the bird more formally known as the American bittern.
146. h. Mourning Cloak is a butterfly.
147. i. Maidenhair Spleenwort is a common fern.
148. f. Bullhead is a fish.
149. c. Woodcock, a bird in the sandpiper family.

150. c. The fringed gentian. We're reminded of William Cullen Bryant's "To the Fringed Gentian":
> "Thou waitest late and com'st alone,
> When woods are bare and birds have flown,
> And frosts and shortening days portend
> The aged year is near its end."
151. b. False
152. b. Valley of Vermont.
153. The male.
154. a. Indiana Bats.
155. b. False (There are timber rattlesnakes, especially in southwestern Vermont.)
156. Robinson
157. d. Johnson—*The Nature of Vermont*
158. a. Thompson—*Natural History of Vermont*
159. e. Aiken—*Pioneering with Wildflowers*
160. b. Klyza and Trombulak—*The Story of Vermont: A Natural and Cultural History*
161. c. Meeks—*Vermont's Land and Resources*
162. c. north.
163. Jack-in-the-Pulpit
164. Ronald Rood of Lincoln
165. c. diving ducks.
166. They are all names of Vermont bogs.
167. George Perkins Marsh (1801–1882). In 1864 he wrote *Man and Nature*.
168. Eastern Mountain Lion—On the list
169. Dutch Elm—Not on the list*
170. Chittenden County—Should be on the list
171. Barn Swallow—Should be on the list**
172. Common Tern—On the list
173. Lake Sturgeon—On the list

*Even though they are almost gone in Vermont, the splitting maul handle and gasoline-driven wood splitter lobbyists are working hard to keep them off the endangered species list.

**The barn swallow lives in barns, good old-fashioned barns with haylofts and timbers and dark dusty corners. We seem to be losing these.

174. Great Blue Heron—Not on the list
175. Fisher Cat—Not on the list
176. Republicans—Should be on the list
177. American Moose—Not on the list
178. Lady Slipper—Not on the list (However, it is on the "Threat-ened List," with a high possibility of becoming endangered in the near future.)
179. Spruce Grouse—On the list
180. Common Loon—On the list
181. Town Meeting—Should be on the list***
182. Bald Eagle—On the list
183. Timber Rattlesnake—On the list
184. Bearberry Willow—On the list
185. Raven—Not on the list
186. Lynx—On the list
187. Skidway Header—Should be on the list****
188. Coydog—Not on the list
189. Spotted Turtle—On the list
190. The Real Vermonter—Should be on the list
191. b. Lake Memphremagog.
192. a. Lake Willoughby

*** We became truly pessimistic about the future of town meeting when a Vermont state senator described in detail and with some fascination a "strange" electoral device he had "discovered" in a town meeting he'd visited recently in one of the smaller towns in his district. It turned out to be the *normal* method of electing officers by ballot during the meeting when a majority is needed to win. When we elect state senators no more familiar with town meeting than that, we'd best get it on the official endangered species list ASAP.

**** You don't roll logs on trucks via a "skidway header" any more. You place them on the truck with a huge device perched on the cab called a (log, wood, apple, cherry) picker. (Answer: cherry)

CHAPTER 4

You Can't Get There From Here*

Vermont Roads

Vermonters are proud of their ability to get around the state. Most of all they cherish their capacity to know direction. They delight in taking the short cut, the back road that "brings them out" just a few miles "above" the village or "below" the Carbee farm. Those who are not capable of driving the state on their own are often forced to stop and ask directions. And you know what that means.*

193. The junction of Routes 11, 30, and 7A in Manchester is known locally as

    a. Petticoat Junction.
    b. Railroad Junction.
    c. Malfunction Junction.
    d. Extreme Junction.

194. I-91 and I-89 intersect in the town of

    a. Norwich.
    b. Hartford.
    c. Windsor.
    d. Sharon.

195. If you head east from Route 100 in Rochester over the "Bethel Mountain Road" and turn right when you "come out," in what town do you end up?

*See the story at the end of the question section on page 43.

196. To go from Bentley's restaurant in Woodstock to Barnard, take

   a. Route 4
   b. Route 12.
   c. Route 106.
   d. None of the above.

197. If you stick to state and/or federal highways, which two locations are the furthest apart?

   a. Springfield and Bellows Falls
   b. Londonderry and Weston
   c. Bradford and Newbury
   d. Burlington and Montpelier

198. Routes 15 and 104 intersect in the town of

   a. Cambridge.
   b. Morrisville.
   c. Manchester.
   d. Rutland.

199. Traveling on Route 12A from Cornish, New Hampshire, you can cross the Connecticut River via the longest double-span covered bridge in the world into the town of

   a. Bellows Falls.
   b. Putney.
   c. Windsor.
   d. Hartland.

200. If you are on Route 15 heading east from Jeffersonville to West Danville, which of the following locations is *not* on the way?

   a. Wolcott
   b. Hardwick
   c. Johnson
   d. Elmore
   e. All of the above

201. The principal north-south highway in Grand Isle County is

    a. Route 2.
    b. Route 7.
    c. Route 108.
    d. I-91.

202. To get from Guildhall to Island Pond, go _____ on Route 102 to _____ and then _____ on Route _____.

    a. south / Lunenburg / west / 2.
    b. east / Bloomfield / north / 105.
    c. north / Bloomfield / west / 105.
    d. north / Lyndonville / east / 114.

203. You are traveling south on Route 5A. Soon after Routes 58 and 16 connect from the west, a long lake parallels the highway on your right. What is its name?

    a. Lake Memphremagog
    b. Crystal Lake
    c. Lake Bomoseen
    d. Lake Willoughby

204. Before the interstate, this was the primary north-south route from Brattleboro to Newport.

    a. Route 5
    b. Route 30
    c. Route 302
    d. Route 7

Match the highway with its other name:

205. _____ Route 302   a. Calvin Coolidge Memorial Highway

206. _____ Route 15   b. Grand Army of the Republic Highway

207. _____ Route 132   c. Theodore Roosevelt Highway

208. _____ Route 2   d. William Scott Memorial Highway

209. _____ Route 103   e. Justin Smith Morrill Highway

"Gaps," "Gorges," and "Gulfs." Match the geological phenomenon with the highway you'd be on as you passed through it.

210. _____ Appalachian Gap   a. Route 100

211. _____ Granville Gulf   b. Route 4

212. _____ Quechee Gorge   c. Route 17

213. _____ Middlebury Gap   d. Route 14

214. _____ Williamstown Gulf   e. Route 12

215. _____ Hubbardton Gulf   f. Route 125

216. _____ Brookfield Gulf   g. Route 30

Find the route that will take you across Vermont's border into one of our neighboring states or Canada.

217. _____ Canada   a. Route 74

218. _____ New Hampshire   b. Route 8

219. _____ Massachusetts   c. Route 108

220. _____ New York   d. Route 25

221. It is where the towns of Montgomery, Westfield, and Lowell come together. Route 58 goes through it now. A famous military road was the first to use it and there is a marker there commemorating the older highway. It is?

222. To enjoy some professional theatre productions, go to the newly restored Dorset Playhouse on

    a. Route 30.

    b. Route 7.

    c. Route 11.

    d. Route 4.

223. If you head east from Route 16 in Greensboro Bend over the "Stannard Mountain Road" and keep going until you "come out," in what town will you arrive?

224. Heading south on Route 100 towards Weston Village you encounter a 7-mile humpback in the road known as

    a. "Terrible Mountain."
    b. "The Long Climb."
    c. "Rocky Road."
    d. "The 7-Mile Humpback."

225. The historic Crown Point Road followed which route?

    a. Route 5 through St. Johnsbury
    b. Route 105 through North Troy
    c. Route 103 through Ludlow
    d. Route 30 through Townshend

226. The John H. Boylan State Airport is located on which road? Hint: This is also a great road for spotting moose.

    a. Route 30
    b. Route 9
    c. Route 114
    d. Route 105

227. You're in Harmonyville. You're between

    a. Jamaica and Rawsonville.
    b. Grafton and Chester.
    c. Chester and Springfield.
    d. Newfane and Townshend.

228. The Green Mountain Railroad operates a scenic 13-mile railroad trip which includes the Brockway Mills Gorge between

    a. St. Albans and Sheldon Springs.
    b. Richmond and Waterbury.
    c. Manchester and Arlington.
    d. Chester and Bellows Falls.

229. Lyndon State College is located just off

    a. I-89.
    b. I-91.
    c. Route 2.
    d. Route 302.

230. Route 9 between Brattleboro and Bennington is also called

    a. the Bayley-Hazen Military road.
    b. the Molly Stark Trail.
    c. the Appalachian Trail.
    d. the Long Trail.

231. You are in Rutland and you need to get to Castleton State College. Which road do you take?

    a. Route 4
    b. Route 7
    c. Route 22A
    d. Route 133

232. On the road to Lincoln is a very popular swimming spot on the New Haven River in Bristol called

    a. Lord's Prayer Falls.
    b. Lincoln Falls.
    c. Bartlett's Falls.
    d. New Haven Falls.

233. If you are driving on Vermont's Skyline Drive, you would be on Mount _____.

234. Above is a crossroads in Chittenden County. It is located in the town of _____.

235. This Vermont crossroads is located in the city of _____.

236. Can you identify the town in which this crossroads is
     located?

*Just about the time you think you've heard all the "how do you get
to" jokes, you run into another. How about this one that appears in
Judson Hale's *Inside New England*. We have quoted it word for word
from Hale's book:

> Writer Bill Conklin tells a true "asking directions" story
> that occurred several years ago when he was moving from "away"
> to the town of Walpole, New Hampshire. He'd somehow
> wound up across the Connecticut River from Walpole, in the
> town of Westminster, Vermont, and although he could plainly
> see the church spires of Walpole, he couldn't find the road to
> the bridge that would get him there. Finally, he stopped to
> ask directions. The classic setup.

> "Can you tell me how to get across to Walpole?" he asked
> an elderly gentleman walking along beside the road.

> "Well, turn right a few hundred yards down this road, cross
> the bridge, and you'll be there," the man said in what ap-
> peared to be a very un-Vermontlike response to a tourist ask-
> ing directions, but then, after a short pause, he added, "I
> wouldn't go there, though."

> "Why shouldn't I?" Bill asked, at once apprehensive.

> "Didn't say *you* shouldn't," he replied. "Said *I* wouldn't."

Answers
Vermont Roads

193. c. Malfunction Junction. There is no stop light, and there are lots and lots of pedestrians.
194. b. Hartford.
195. Bethel
196. b. Route 12.
197. d. Burlington and Montpelier
198. a. Cambridge.
199. c. Windsor.
200. d. Elmore
201. a. Route 2.
202. c. north / Bloomfield / west / 105.
203. d. Lake Willoughby
204. a. Route 5
205. d. William Scott Memorial Highway. Private William Scott fell asleep on guard duty during the Civil War. (He had taken a sick friend's shift the night before.) Ordered to be shot by firing squad, he was spared by Abraham Lincoln in a celebrated case. But Scott was never to return to his homeland hills of Groton. He was killed during a charge at Lee's Mill, Virginia.
206. b. Grand Army of the Republic Highway
207. e. Justin Smith Morrill Highway
208. c. Theodore Roosevelt Highway
209. a. Calvin Coolidge Memorial Highway
210. c. Route 17
211. a. Route 100
212. b. Route 4
213. f. Route 125
214. d. Route 14
215. g. Route 30
216. e. Route 12
217. c. Route 108 (at Berkshire)
218. d. Route 25 (at Bradford)

219. b. Route 8 (at Stamford)
220. a. Route 74 (at Shoreham)
221. Hazen's Notch. The military road was called the Bayley-Hazen Road. It began in Newbury.
222. a. Route 30.
223. Nope, not Stannard. You'll be in Lyndon.
224. a. "Terrible Mountain."
225. c. Route 103 through Ludlow
226. d. Route 105 (in Island Pond)
227. d. Newfane and Townshend.
228. d. Chester and Bellows Falls.
229. b. I-91
230. b. the Molly Stark Trail.
231. a. Route 4
232. c. Bartlett's Falls.
233. Equinox (Opened in the summer of 1947, Skyline Drive travels to the top of Big Equinox, 3,816 feet above sea level. It is between 6 and 7 miles long.)
234. Essex Junction
235. Rutland
236. Manchester

THE NEW HAMPSHIRE PAGES

"Anything I can say about New Hampshire can be said as well about Vermont. Excepting that they differ in their mountains. The Vermont mountains stretch extended straight; New Hampshire mountains (237.) _____ _____ _____ _____ _____ *."*

–Robert Frost

Vermonters have always claimed an ability to tell the difference between Vermont and New Hampshire. Indeed, the differences are many. But often it takes a well-honed Vermont consciousness to detect them. They are not all as blatant, for instance, as the presidential election of 1840 when Vermonters voted for Harrison two-to-one, while across the river our New England neighbors in New Hampshire voted three-to-one for Van Buren. Historian of the period Richard P. McCormick called it a "conundrum." The following questions test your knowledge of Vermont and New Hampshire as a pair of very different oxen that (as Robert Frost said) share a geographical yoke—the back country of the Northeast.

Which State?	VT	NH
238. Has the higher percent of adults who smoke?	_____	_____
239. Files more bankruptcies?	_____	_____
240. Has higher *per capita* alcohol consumption?	_____	_____
241. Has higher percent of sunny days?	_____	_____
242. Has more miles of coastline?	_____	_____
243. Is geographically larger?	_____	_____
244. Contains Mt. Lafayette?	_____	_____
245. Has higher mountains?	_____	_____
246. Puts more miles on its cars?	_____	_____
247. Spends more per pupil for education?	_____	_____
248. Voted for Roosevelt in 1936?	_____	_____
249. Has more doctors per 1000 residents?	_____	_____

250. Had the higher percent of population increase for the 1990-2000 decade? _____ _____

251. Has the higher percentage of population having completed 4 or more years of college? _____ _____

252. Has the larger state legislature? _____ _____

253. Has an Ivy League college? _____ _____

254. Is the home of *Yankee* magazine? _____ _____

255. Produces more eggs? _____ _____

256. Has Bretton Woods? _____ _____

257. Contains Caledonia County? _____ _____

258. Has more farms? _____ _____

259. Has the higher crime rate? _____ _____

260. Has the higher suicide rate? _____ _____

261. Has more women than men? _____ _____

Answers
The New Hampshire Pages

237. *curl up in a coil*
238. New Hampshire
239. New Hampshire
240. New Hampshire is ranked first in the nation. (Of course it might be the case that lots of out-of-staters travel to New Hampshire to buy their liquor.)
241. New Hampshire with 55% compared to Vermont's 44%.
242. New Hampshire. Vermont doesn't have a coastline!
243. Vermont has almost 300 more square miles.
244. New Hampshire
245. New Hampshire. Mt. Washington at 6,288 feet is nearly two thousand feet higher than Vermont's Mount Mansfield.
246. Vermont with 13,267 miles per year as opposed to New Hampshire's 11,318.
247. Vermont
248. New Hampshire
249. Vermont
250. New Hampshire
251. Vermont
252. New Hampshire has the largest of any state: 400 in the House and 24 in the Senate. Vermont has 150 in the House and 30 in the Senate.
253. New Hampshire. Dartmouth College. The University of Vermont must be satisfied with its informal categorization as a "public ivy."
254. *Yankee* is published in Dublin, New Hampshire.
255. Vermont
256. New Hampshire. This resort is in the White Mountains on Route 302.
257. Vermont
258. Vermont has more than double.
259. Vermont
260. New Hampshire
261. Both do.

CHAPTER 5

The 251 Club

Vermont Towns

In Vermont towns lies the spirit of public life. Even though some of our towns have become cities, we are still apt to think of them the old way, as towns. There is even a club in Vermont made up of persons who have visited all of Vermont's cities and towns (and even some places that used to be towns). Our towns reflect our history. They are a compass to travel by. They sponsor our cherished political structure—town meeting. Often their names are unique and colorful.

262. Speaking of color, there is only one town whose name is (in total) a color of the spectrum. Can you name it?

263. Which town is the most likely to have been the first town in Vermont inhabited by human beings?
    a. Sutton
    b. Coventry
    c. Troy
    d. Swanton

264. What town is the site of Vermont's only nuclear power plant?

265. _____ and 266. _____ are the only two Vermont towns with the name of an American state.

Two towns, 267. _____ and 268. _____ have
the name of a capital of a foreign country* and nine have the
names of capitals of American states:

269. _____, 270. _____,
271. _____, 272. _____,
273. _____, 274. _____,
275. _____, 276._____,
and 277. _____.

278. Many towns are named the same as very big cities outside
Vermont. What is the largest American city that has the
same name as a Vermont town?

Four Vermont towns have names that remind us of biblical times.
Name them.

279. _____, 280. _____
281. _____, 282. _____

Some towns remind one of England and our British heritage.
Burke, Vermont, for instance, has the same name as an important English political philosopher. Can you name the Vermont
towns that have the same name as a:

283. British general in World War II?   _____
284. major British university?   _____
285. famous English 17th century poet?   _____

The name of some Vermont towns can be associated with posi-
tion, such as *Top*sham. Name four others that either begin or
end with *under, over, high,* or *low* as separate syllable(s)—that is,
S*under*land, Gl*over*, D*over*, Bel*low*s Falls, and *Low*ell would not
count:

Under and *Over*	*High* and *Low*
286. _____	288. _____
287. _____	289. _____

*Nope, it is not Moscow. Moscow, Vermont, is not a town. Nor is it
a village. It is, like "Beecher Falls," just a place.

What about towns that used to be? One had the same name as a famous bull, 290. _____. Another, the middle name of an author, 291. W. _____ Maugham, and another the last name of a great heavyweight boxer, 292. _____.

Directions on the compass are traditionally associated with place names, such as East Haven and Northfield. In Vermont, however, "West" is most commonly used. Complete the following lists:

Single-word towns incorporating "West" (such as Weston)	*Double-word towns incorporating 'West' (such as West Windsor)*
293. _____	297. _____
294. _____	298. _____
295. _____	299. _____
296. _____	

300. Several Vermont towns have the same names as former governors. Chittenden and Proctor are examples. Of the several that remain, name one.

Some Vermont towns have the names of foreign countries like, for instance, Jamaica. Two others are 301._____ and 302. _____.

303. What town is named for the general who was victorious at the Battle of Bennington?
    a. Starksboro
    b. Bennington
    c. Cabot
    d. Morgan

304. What town was believed to be the site of the ancient pine tree with 14 branches used as the original model for the tree depicted on the state seal?

a. Greensboro
b. Arlington
c. Montpelier
d. Grafton

305. In what year did the town of Victory, Vermont, finally get electrical service?

a. 1946
b. 1954
c. 1963

On the following pages are pictures of four Vermont "downtowns." Can you match the photo to the following?

306. _____   a. Barre
307. _____   b. Brattleboro
308. _____   c. Rutland
309. _____   d. St. Albans

306.

307.

308.

309.

Here are photos of four more Vermont downtowns. Can you recognize them?

310. _____   a. Bennington
311. _____   b. Burlington
312. _____   c. Newport
313. _____   d. St. Johnsbury

310.

311.

312.

313.

Answers
Vermont Towns

262. Orange
263. d. Swanton
264. Vernon
265. Georgia
266. Washington
267. Athens (capital of Greece)
268. Berlin (capital of Germany) Many Vermonters may have said Washington. But, technically anyway, we have to concede that Washington, D.C., is not the capital of a *foreign* country.
269. Montgomery (Alabama)
270. Hartford (Connecticut)
271. Dover (Delaware)
272. Springfield (Illinois)
273. Lincoln (Nebraska)
274. Concord (New Hampshire)
275. Albany (New York)
276. Richmond (Virginia)
277. Charleston (West Virginia)
278. Baltimore
279. Jericho
280. Eden
281. Canaan
282. Goshen
283. Montgomery
284. Cambridge
285. Milton
286. *Under*hill
287. And*over*
288. *High*gate
289. Lud*low*
290. Ferdinand
291. Somerset
292. Lewis

293. Westmore
294. Westfield
295. Westford
296. Westminster
297. West Fairlee
298. West Haven
299. West Rutland
300. Fletcher, Johnson, or Woodbury
301. Peru
302. Holland. OK, so Holland isn't technically a country; it's a province of the Netherlands. Most Vermonters know Holland as that nice country in Europe with the windmills and tulips. Close enough.
303. a. Starksboro
304. b. Arlington (but it blew down many years ago.)
305. c. 1963
306. c. Rutland
307. a. Barre
308. d. St. Albans
309. b. Brattleboro
310. c. Newport
311. a. Bennington
312. b. Burlington
313. d. St. Johnsbury

LIFESTYLES OF THE RICH AND/OR FAMOUS PAGES

Match the movie with the Vermont town where much or some of the filming took place:

_____314. *Funny Farm* (Chevy Chase)   a. Peacham
_____315. *Baby Boom* (Diane Keaton)   b. Dummerston
_____316. *The Cider House Rules*   c. Manchester
        (Michael Caine)
_____317. *The Spitfire Grill* (Ellen Burstyn) d. Grafton

The following matching items make sense because of a famous person:

_____318. Thetford   a. *The Jungle Book*
_____319. Dummerston   b. "Little Boy Blue"
_____320. Barnard   c. *Elmer Gantry*
_____321. Newfane   d. Wells-Fargo

Match the town with the famous person:

_____322. Tantoo Cardinal   a. Bennington
_____323. Grandma Moses   b. Bethel
_____324. Anne Morrow Lindbergh   c. Dorset
_____325. Admiral George Dewey   d. Danby
_____326. Justice William Rehnquist   e. Greensboro
_____327. John Irving   f. Passumpsic
_____328. Pearl Buck   g. Montpelier
_____329. Vilhjamur Stefansson   h. Lyndonville

330. The Rockefeller family is associated with the town of
_____.

331. One of the most significant writers of the twentieth century lived for many years in Cavendish, Vermont. His name is _____.

332. One of America's best-known novelists taught for years at Bennington College. He died in 1986. His name was _____.

333. Maria von Trapp, who operated the Trapp Family Lodge in Stowe, reminds us immediately of the movie classic _____.

334. Which of the following movies was *not* filmed in Vermont?
    a. *What Lies Beneath* (Harrison Ford, Michele Pfeiffer)
    b. *Me, Myself, and Irene* (Jim Carrey, Renee Zellwegger)
    c. *Downhill Racer* (Robert Redford)
    d. *Stranger in the Kingdom* (Martin Sheen)

Perhaps the most famous scene ever filmed in Vermont starred (335.) _____ in the movie (336.) _____.
It was filmed on the (337.) _____ River.

338. Identify this photo. Hint: It was the summer home of Robert Todd Lincoln.

Answers
Rich and/or Famous Pages

314. d. Grafton

315. c. Manchester

316. b. Dummerston

317. a. Peacham (Peacham was also used for the filming of *Ethan Frome* with Liam Neeson.)

318. d. Henry Wells of Thetford was the Wells of the Wells-Fargo Company.

319. a. Rudyard Kipling wrote both *The Jungle Book* and *Captains Courageous* in Dummerston.

320. c. Sinclair Lewis, author of *Elmer Gantry* and *Babbitt*, called Barnard, Vermont, "One of the few decent places in America to live."

321. b. Eugene Field, author of "Little Boy Blue" and called the "poet of American childhood," played on the green in Newfane as a boy.

322. h. Actress Tantoo Cardinal (*Dances With Wolves*) lives in Lyndonville.

323. a. Grandma Moses lived for a time in Bennington. In addition, the schoolhouse that she attended as a child in Eagle Bridge, New York, was eventually relocated to Bennington.

324. f. Anne Morrow, writer and wife of aviator Charles Lindbergh, lived in Passumpsic. Their daughter Reeve Tripp still lives there.

325. g. Dewey, the Admiral of Manila Bay grew up across from the capitol building in Montpelier. (You didn't confuse him with Burlington's John Dewey, the famous philosopher and educator, did you?)

326. e. Greensboro, Vermont's Caspian Lake is a great gathering point for the rich and famous, including Bernard DeVoto and Chief Justice Rehnquist.

327. c. John Irving, author of *Cider House Rules, The World According to Garp,* and other novels resides in Dorset.

328. d. The author of the *Good Earth*, Pearl Buck lived in Danby.

329. b. Polar explorer Vilhjamur Stefansson had a summer home in Bethel.
330. Woodstock
331. Aleksandr Solzhenitsyn (He eventually returned to his homeland of Russia.)
332. Bernard Malamud (author of *A New Life* and *The Natural*)
333. *The Sound of Music*
334. c. *Downhill Racer*
335. Lillian Gish
336. *Way Down East*
337. White
338. Hildene in Manchester

CHAPTER 6

Who Are Those Folks, Anyway?

Many have tried to map that rugged territory called the Vermont "character." Its precise dimensions remain a mystery, yet the general contours are everywhere evident. They are contained in the notions of liberty spawned in and by community, the courage and wisdom to take democracy seriously, personal independence and self-reliance, a faith in the work ethic, and fidelity to the truth that every individual is a free person with the right to be a saint or a damned fool. This capacity for free will, believe Vermonters, radiates a special dignity reserved only for the human race.

The 50 people listed below—some living, some dead, some born in Vermont, others not—all share in some respect a common denominator spelled V-E-R-M-O-N-T-E-R. We have clustered them in five groups of ten and simply ask you to match their names with the characteristics with which they are associated.

Group A

_____	339. Allen R. Foley	a. Auctioneer
_____	340. Marselis Parsons	b. Logger
_____	341. Hamilton Davis	c. Bureaucrat, Conservationist
_____	342. Jody Williams	d. Humorist, Professor
_____	343. Perry Merrill	e. Author, Journalist
_____	344. Harland Tatro	f. Printmaker
_____	345. Deborah Clifford	g. Newspaper Editor
_____	346. M. Dickey Drysdale	h. News Anchor
_____	347. Lawrence Felion	i. Historian, Vermont Women
_____	348. Mary Azarian	j. Nobel Peace Prize

Group B

_____ 349. Weston Cate   a. Super Athlete

_____ 350. Libby Smith   b. Old-time Fiddler

_____ 351. Bill Tabor   c. Vermont Supreme Court Justice

_____ 352. Marilyn Skoglund   d. The Logger

_____ 353. David Mason   e. Vermont Country Store

_____ 354. Vrest Orton   f. Chief, Abenaki Tribe

_____ 355. Rusty DeWees   g. Ox Teamster

_____ 356. Blanche H. Moyse   h. Former Vermont Historical Society Director

_____ 357. Homer St. Francis   i. Promoter of Classical Music, Windham County

_____ 358. Wilfred Guillette   j. Stone Wall Builder

Group C

_____ 359. D. Gregory Sanford   a. Man with a Plan

_____ 360. Maxine Brandenburg   b. Poet

_____ 361. Dorothy Canfield Fisher   c. Novelist, Conservationist

_____ 362. Daisy Dopp   d. Columnist in the Kingdom

_____ 363. Harold Blaisdell   e. Legislator, Bureaucrat

_____ 364. Richard Mallary   f. Town Manager, Brattleboro

_____ 365. Caroline A. Yale   g. Educating the Deaf

_____ 366. Jerry Remillard   h. Outdoorsman, Writer

_____ 367. Fred Tuttle   i. State Archivist, Historian

_____ 368. John Engels   j. Vermont Business Roundtable

Group D

_____ 369. Peter Jennison   a   Keeping Track of Wildlife

_____ 370. Susan Morse   b.   Eco-Libertarian

_____ 371. Walter Hard   c.   IDX CEO

_____ 372. Murray Bookchin   d.   Vermont Historian: Place-Names

_____ 373. John McClaughry   e.   Literary Critic, Poet, Orleans

_____ 374. Christopher Bohjalian   f.   Author, Conservative Political Activist

_____ 375. Jim Hayford   g.   _Midwives_

_____ 376. Esther Swift   h.   Schoolteacher

_____ 377. Esther J. Urie   i.   Writer, Founder of Countryman Press

_____ 378. Richard Tarrant   j.   Poet of the Vermont Character

Group E

_____ 379. Bill Mares   a.   Filmmaker, Peacham Resident

_____ 380. Lola Aiken   b.   Pulitzer Prize Winner

_____ 381. Deborah Markowitz   c.   Novelist

_____ 382. Ruth Page   d.   First Lady of Vermont

_____ 383. Bonny Reynolds   e.   Author, School Teacher

_____ 384. Ely Culbertson   f.   "Bridge for Peace"

_____ 385. Mrs. Lisle McIntosh   g.   Town Clerk

_____ 386. David Moats   h.   Vermont Public Radio

_____ 387. Howard Mosher   i.   Secretary of State

_____ 388. Jay Craven   j.   Mincemeat Maker

Answers
Who Are Those Folks, Anyway?

Group A

339. d. Allen R. Foley
     Humorist, professor at Dartmouth, author of *What the Old-Timer Said.*

340. h. Marselis Parsons
     Journalist, longtime news anchor for WCAX-TV.

341. e. Hamilton Davis
     Author, journalist, consultant, and public policy guru.

342. j. Jody Williams
     From Putney, Vermont, she received the Nobel Peace Prize in 1997 for her efforts in the banning and clearing of anti-personnel mines.

343. c. Perry Merrill
     Bureaucrat, conservationist, author.

344. a. Harland Tatro
     Auctioneer, Alburg.

345. i. Deborah Clifford
     Historian, scholar of political activism among Vermont women.

346. g. M. Dickey Drysdale
     Editor of the *White River Valley Herald* newspaper in Randolph.

347. b. Lawrence Felion
     One of Vermont's most famous loggers, Leicester. "Tweeter" and his son "Homer" have been logging with the same skidder for over 30 years.

348. f. Mary Azarian
     Printmaker, Plainfield. She created *A Farmer's Alphabet* and *The Tale of John Barleycorn.*

Group B

349. h. Weston Cate
     Director, Vermont Historical Society, January, 1975–August, 1985. Past moderator, Town of East Montpelier, and real Vermonter extraordinaire.
350. a. Libby Smith
     Super athlete—golf *and* basketball.
351. g. Bill Tabor
     Ox teamster in Cuttingsville.
352. c. Marilyn Skoglund
     Vermont Supreme Court Justice.
353. j. David Mason
     Builds stone walls by hand. *Vermont Life* did an award-winning profile on "Stoney" Mason of Starksboro.
354. e. Vrest Orton
     Founder, Vermont Country Store.
355. d. Rusty DeWees
     Entertains audiences with his one-man show *The Logger*.
356. i. Blanche Honegger Moyse
     Promoter of classical music, Windham County. She also helped found the famous Marlboro Festival of Music along with Rudolf Serkin, and Louis and Marcel Moyse.
357. f. Homer St. Francis
     Chief, Abenaki Indian tribe. Died in 2001.
358. b. Wilfred Guillette
     Old-time fiddler, carpenter, from Derby.

Group C

359. i. D. Gregory Sanford
     State archivist and distinguished historian.
360. j. Maxine Brandenburg
     President of the Vermont Business Roundtable.
361. c. Dorothy Canfield Fisher
     Writer, novelist, conservationist.

362. d. Daisy Dopp
Northeast Kingdom newspaper columnist. Elka Schumann calls her "one of the memorable citizens of Vermont's Northeast Kingdom."

363. h. Harold Blaisdell
He was one of Vermont's best-known outdoorsmen. He wrote four books on fishing in Vermont, including *The Philosophical Fisherman* and *Tricks That Take Fish*.

364. e. Richard Mallary
Politician, farmer, public administrator, from Fairlee.

365. g. Caroline A. Yale
World leader in education for the deaf. Born in Charlotte, she served for fifty years as head of the Clarke School for the Deaf in Northampton, Massachusetts. Caroline Sweet of Woodstock and Gertrude Croker of Brattleboro were also known for their work in education for the deaf.

366. f. Jerry Remillard
Town manager, Brattleboro.

367. a. Fred Tuttle
Star of the quirky movie *The Man With the Plan*.

368. b. John Engels
Vermont poet, professor of English at St. Michael's College. His books of verse include *The Seasons in Vermont* and *The Homer Mitchell Place*.

Group D

369. i. Peter Jennison
Writer, founder of the Countryman Press.

370. a. Susan Morse
Her *Keeping Track* project has citizens recording data and learning more about the wildlife of Vermont.

371. j. Walter Hard
Vermont poet, known for his descriptions of Vermont people and as owner of the Johnny Appleseed Bookshop in Manchester. When he died at age 84 he had written nine volumes of poetry and two of prose.

372. b. Murray Bookchin
     Eco-libertarian, author and scholar, Burlington.
373. f. John McClaughry
     Author, commentator, conservative political activist, and
     town moderator in Kirby.
374. g. Christopher Bohjalian
     Author from Lincoln whose *Midwives* was an Oprah's Book
     Club selection. Other works include *Trans-Sister Radio* and
     Water Witches.
375. e. Jim Hayford
     Poet, schoolteacher, literary critic from Orleans.
376. d. Esther Swift
     Vermont historian from Royalton. A sixth-generation Ver-
     monter who wrote, among other volumes, *Vermont Place-
     Names*, a prodigious effort in the Vermont tradition of
     painstaking care and excellence.
377. h. Esther J. Urie
     Prominent Vermont schoolteacher for forty years.
378. c. Richard Tarrant
     St. Michael's College alumnus now serving as CEO of IDX.

Group E

379. e. Bill Mares
     Author, school teacher, man of letters, Burlington. If you
     like fishing or beer, pick up his *Fishing with the Presidents*
     and *Making Beer*. You might also enjoy *Real Vermonters
     Don't Milk Goats* and *The Vermont Owner's Manual* that
     he co-authored with some guy named Bryan.
380. d. Lola Aiken
     "First Lady of Vermont." Wife of former senator George
     Aiken.
381. i. Deborah Markowitz
     First female *elected* Secretary of State in Vermont. Helen
     Burbank was *appointed* in 1947 when Rawson Myrick re-
     signed.
382. h. Ruth Page
     Commentator for Vermont Public Radio. Former co-pub-

lisher of the *Essex Reporter,* garden specialist, and environmentalist.

383. g. Bonny Reynolds
Town Clerk in Springfield.

384. f. Ely Culbertson
"Bridge for Peace." He lived in Barnard, Vermont. His books on bridge (the card game) were the best-selling nonfiction books in America next to the Bible in the 1930s and 1940s. As a major force in the peace movement of his day and head of the Citizens Committee for United Nations Reform, he fought for world disarmament and control of atomic weapons.

385. j. Mrs. Lisle McIntosh
Mincemeat maker of South Royalton. She became a legend throughout New England. In 1950 at the age of 86 she "put up" 4½ tons of mincemeat, got into a truck, and sold it on the road for cash.

386. b. David Moats
Pulitzer prize winner for editorials on civil unions.

387. c. Howard Mosher
Novelist. If you wonder why Ken Kesey (*One Flew Over the Cuckoo's Nest* and *Sometimes a Great Notion*) has said of Mosher's *Disappearances* ". . . one hell of a book! A wonderful book, a terrible book. It touches the vein of Hawthorne and Poe, running deep in the American fear and the American hope," then read how Howard Mosher finishes a story. From his novel about life in the Northeast Kingdom, *Disappearances*: "The sun was rising, glinting off Rene's musket, shining on the snow, illuminating the swamp, Kingdom County, Vermont and Quebec. Downriver a loon hooted, its long wild call floated over the water and trees and snow as I stood with empty arms on the edge of my youth in a place wheeling sunward, full of terror, full of wonder."

388. a. Jay Craven
Filmmaker, Kingdom County Productions. Films include *Where the Rivers Flow North, A Stranger in the Kingdom,* and *Disappearances.*

THE CATEGORY IS VERMONT

Anyone who has watched some of the newly popular quiz shows must have noticed that Vermont turns up quite often as an answer. Here is a pure Vermont version of one of America's favorite real quiz shows. (For those who don't know how to play, below are answers. Your job: supply the questions to them. The category is Vermont.)

First Round

389. The state beverage
390. V.A.S.T.
391. First Tuesday in March
392. The honeybee
393. Twelve days before Thanksgiving
394. The state horse
395. Champ
396. Eight-zero-two
397. Hermit Thrush
398. The WCAX-TV farm and home show hosted by Tony Adams
399. The Bennington Mob
400. The 251 Club
401. Vermont's fifth season
402. (visual clue below) Randolph, Vermont

Second Round

403. Number of cities in the state
404. The highest grade of maple syrup
405. Suicide Six
406. The weed invading many of Vermont's lakes and streams
407. Brattleboro, Dover, Stratton, and Westminster, for example
408. The state mineral
409. Page, Jon, Mike and Trey
410. Grand Isle, Burlington, and Charlotte
411. Four feet by four feet by eight feet
412. Canaan
413. *Universitas Viridis Montis*
414. It is comprised of the counties of Orleans, Essex, and Caledonia
415. The birthplace of Vermont
416. Cohen and Greenfield
417. Ethan Allen's second wife

The Tie-Breaker

418. One percent of the total assessed valuation of all real estate or personal property in a town

Answers
The Category Is Vermont

First Round

389. What is milk?
390. What is the Vermont Association of Snow Travelers?
391. What is Town Meeting Day?
392. What is the state insect?
393. What is the start of deer season with firearms?
394. What is the Morgan?
395. What is the name of Lake Champlain's answer to the Loch Ness Monster or the Vermont Expos mascot?
396. What is the telephone area code for the entire state of Vermont?
397. What is the state bird?
398. What is *Across the Fence*?
399. What did the Yorkers call the Green Mountain Boys?
400. What club's members visit all of Vermont's cities, towns, and gores?
401. What is mud season?
402. The whale tails in the photograph were moved to this South Burlington location from what New England town?

Second Round

403. What is nine? (Barre, Burlington, Montpelier, Newport, Rutland, Saint Albans, South Burlington, Vergennes, Winooski)
404. What is fancy?
405. What is the name of a ski area in Woodstock?
406. What is Eurasian milfoil?
407. What are towns in Windham County?
408. What is talc?
409. Who are the members of the band Phish? (Page McConnell, Jon Fishman, Mike Gordon, and Trey Anastasio—originally a Burlington-based band—experienced a meteoric rise to fame.)

410. What are the three Lake Champlain ferry crossings in Vermont?
411. What are the dimensions of a cord of wood?
412. What is the most northern and eastern town in Vermont?
413. What is the Latin for University of the Green Mountains, from which the abbreviation UVM was formed?
414. What is the Northeast Kingdom?
415. What is Windsor called? (Where in 1777 Vermont was declared an independent republic.)
416. Who were the originators of Ben & Jerry's ice cream? (Ben Cohen and Jerry Greenfield)
417. Who was Fanny Montresor Buchanan Allen?

Tie-Breaker

418. What is the Grand List?

CHAPTER 7

The Old Stone House

Vermont Landmarks

In Vermont most anything can be a landmark. We even passed "landmark" legislation (the billboard law) so we could see them better. People are landmarks. Stores are landmarks. Farms are landmarks. It's easier to proclaim things like these landmarks in Vermont since people and stores and farms tend to stay put longer here. Below are .000076% of Vermont's landmarks with our apologies to the others that we (of course) considered but left out.

419. The Old Stone House was originally built as a school dormitory by Reverend Alexander Lucius Twilight, the first African American in America to receive a college degree. Where is it located?

Match the landmark to the town:

_____ 420. American Precision Museum   a. Alburg

_____ 421. Joe's Pond   b. Bristol

_____ 422. Ben & Jerry's   c. Cabot and
         Manufacturing Plant   Danville

_____ 423. The Athenaeum   d. Charlotte

_____ 424. Vermont Wildflower Farm   e. Danby

_____ 425. The Alburg Auction House   f. Essex Junction

_____ 426. Eureka Schoolhouse   g. Ferrisburg
         (oldest in Vermont)

_____ 427. Green Mountain Audubon   h. Huntington
         Nature Center

_____ 428. Button Bay State Park   i. Middlebury

_____ 429. The Vermont Country Store   j. Middlesex

_____ 430. The Morgan Horse Farm   k. Pittsford

_____ 431. The Discovery Museum   l. St. Johnsbury

_____ 432. Polka Dot Diner   m. Sharon

_____ 433. Lord's Prayer Rock   n. Springfield

_____ 434. Wrightsville Dam   o. Waterbury

_____ 435. New England Maple Museum   p. Weston and
                                                 Rockingham

_____ 436. Peel Gallery of Fine Art   q. Weybridge

_____ 437. Brooksies Restaurant   r. White River
                                                 Junction

_____ 438. Middle Bridge   s. Windsor
         (newest covered bridge)

_____ 439. Pulp Mill Bridge   t. Woodstock
         (oldest covered bridge)

440. The house where President Calvin Coolidge was born is
found in

     a. Ludlow.
     b. Wilmington.
     c. Stratton.
     d. Plymouth.

Name the town where the following landmarks are located:

441. Stone Village   _____

442. Smuggler's Notch   _____

443. Pavilion Office Building   _____

444. The *Ticonderoga*   _____

445. Rock of Ages Quarry   _____

446. Santa's Land   _____

447. The Scott Covered Bridge   _____
     over the West River

448. The Floating Bridge   _____

449. Identify the statue on the Capitol dome in Montpelier.

    a. A cow
    b. Thomas Chittenden
    c. The Goddess of Agriculture
    d. Ethan Allen

450. Dedicated in 1890 by Franklin Fairbanks and containing a planetarium, 19th century treasures, over 150,000 objects from nature and cultures, among other exhibits, the Fairbanks Museum is found in

    a. Brattleboro.
    b. White River Junction.
    c. Winooski.
    d. St. Johnsbury.

451. The Fisher Covered Bridge, spanning the Lamoille River, is the last railroad covered bridge still in use in the country. It is located in

    a. Johnson.
    b. Wolcott.
    c. Hyde Park.
    d. Hardwick.

452. The Bennington Battle Monument commemorates a battle fought in

   a. Bennington, Vermont.
   b. Bennington, New York.
   c. Hoosick Falls, New York.
   d. Manchester, Vermont.

453. The Daniel Webster Monument is located in

   a. Stratton.
   b. Arlington.
   c. Wilmington.
   d. Maine.

454. The Norman Rockwell Exhibit is located in

   a. Burlington.
   b. Manchester.
   c. Arlington.
   d. Rutland.

455. The homestead of Chester A. Arthur, 21st President of the U.S., is in

   a. Bellows Falls.
   b. Fairfield.
   c. Fairfax.
   d. Fair Haven.

456. In Sharon there is a monument and museum, open year-round, memorializing the birthplace of the founder of one of America's important religions, the _____.

457. What is Mount Independence in Orwell named for?

   a. Vermont Independence Day
   b. The U.S. Declaration of Independence
   c. The capture of Fort Ticonderoga
   d. Washington's victory at Yorktown

458. Whose statue is on the portico of the statehouse?

459. Sand Bar State Park is located in
  a. Milton.
  b. South Hero.
  c. Colchester.
  d. Isle La Motte.

460. In Derby, Vermont, there is something strange about the Haskell Opera House. What is it?
  a. It floats.
  b. It is built in a tree.
  c. Audiences sit in the U.S. and watch performers in Canada.
  d. It's haunted.

461. Where is the Justin Morrill homestead?

Match the following with the town:

_____ 462. Park-McCullough Mansion   a. Whitingham
_____ 463. Justin Morgan's burial place   b. North Bennington
_____ 464. Birthplace of Brigham Young   c. Randolph

465. Pictured above is the "Round" Church in Richmond. How many sides does it have?

466. This is the tallest man-made structure in the state of Vermont, standing over 306 feet tall. It is actually made from New York dolomite. What does it commemorate?

467. The nation's oldest log cabin, the Hyde Log Cabin (shown above), is located where?

468. In what town is the Windham County Courthouse
(shown in the picture above)?

Answers
Vermont Landmarks

419. Brownington
420. s. Windsor
421. c. Cabot and Danville
422. o. Waterbury
423. l. St. Johnsbury
424. d. Charlotte
425. a. Alburg (We figured you'd get this one.)
426. n. Springfield
427. h. Huntington
428. g. Ferrisburg
429. p. Weston and Rockingham
430. q. Weybridge
431. f. Essex Junction
432. r. White River Junction (a village in Hartford)
433. b. Bristol
434. j. Middlesex
435. k. Pittsford
436. e. Danby
437. m. Sharon
438. t. Woodstock
439. i. Middlebury
440. d. Plymouth.
441. Chester
442. Cambridge (Stowe and Jeffersonville were good guesses!)
443. Montpelier
444. Shelburne (specifically, the Shelburne Museum)
445. Barre (more technically, Graniteville)
446. Putney
447. Townshend
448. Brookfield (The bridge is 294 feet long, and floats on 380 polystyrene floats. It originally floated on barrels.)
449. c. Ceres, the Goddess of Agriculture, holding sheaves of wheat. It is carved from white pine from the state of—sorry— Washington.

450. d. St. Johnsbury.
451. b. Wolcott.
452. c. Hoosick Falls, New York (originally the town of Wallomsack). General Stark decided to surprise the British five miles from the supply depot at Bennington.
453. a. Stratton.
454. c. Arlington, where Rockwell lived and worked for many years. Many of his subjects for *Saturday Evening Post* covers were Arlington residents.
455. b. Fairfield.
456. Mormon religion. (Joseph Smith was born in Sharon.)
457. b. The U.S. Declaration of Independence
458. Ethan Allen
459. a. Milton.
460. c. The audience sits in the U.S., while the performers (and stage) are in Canada.
461. Strafford. Senator Justin Morrill served in Congress for nearly forty-four years. As author of the Land Grants Act of 1862, which gave public lands to the agricultural colleges of each state, he is probably the Vermonter with the most buildings named after him in the U.S.
462. b. No. Bennington
463. c. Randolph
464. a. Whitingham
465. The Round Church has 16 sides. There is one side for each man who built it plus the belfry for one man. The seventeen men represented five denominations. And from *School Bells among Green Hills,* a fascinating and valuable edition on education in Vermont by the Vermont Association of Retired Teachers (Essex Publishing Company: Essex Junction, Vermont, 1975), comes this: "In Brookline is the country's only round schoolhouse. It was built in 1822 by a Dr. Wilson, who was actually an infamous highwayman from England, known to his European companions as Thunderbolt. Fearing that the authorities would some day discover his identity, he built his brick schoolhouse in the round so that, from any part of the

schoolroom, he could keep an eye out for approaching danger." At one time Henry Ford offered to buy the Round Church and move it out of state, but Richmond refused to sell.

466. The Battle of Bennington, which, as we all know, took place in Hoosick Falls, New York!

467. Grand Isle

468. Newfane

PUNCH LINE PAGES

To survive among Vermonters, it is imperative to know their humor. As Judson Hale says in his book *Inside New England*, Vermont, like Maine, is a region with a distinctiveness that breeds its own brand of humor. Below we have listed the punch lines of a selection of Vermont jokes. Your task is to supply the story that precedes it. All but two or three are Vermont classics. You should "get" the others too. For more delightful Vermont and New England humor, we suggest Hale's book.

469. "Vermont."

470. "I guess I'd be a Democrat."

471. "Didn't know how fast you could walk."

472. "Back to get more rocks."

473. "Not to me it don't."

474. "You can't get there from here."

475. "Had a truck like that once myself. Got rid of it."

476. "More'n ten year ago."

477. ". . . and three to talk about how good the old one was."

478. "Compared to what?"

479. "Not yet."

480. "Bury him."

481. "Born here."

482. "So far I have to keep my own tom cat."

483. "Always has."

484. "You lose."

485. "In a balloon."

486. ". . . couldn't have stood another of them Vermont winters."

487. ". . . you can come in and wait."

488. "Nope. I'm still on my horse."

489. "I wouldn't start from here."

490. "Sure it is. But any damn fool knows how to get to Poultney."

491. "I've been against every damn one of them."

492. "Yep, but they'll all be gone in the fall."

Answers
Punch Lines

469. What is green and goes backwards?

470. An old Vermonter was visiting a friend in Connecticut, back in the days when Democrats were an endangered species in Vermont. Hearing that the Vermonter was a Republican, someone asked him, "Well, why are you a Republican?" "My father was a Republican," the Vermonter replied. "So was my grandfather and my uncle and I believe my great-grandfather as well." "That's no reason!" exclaimed the Connecticut man. "Why if your daddy had been a horse thief, what would you be then?" "In that case," said the Vermonter . . .

471. An out-of-stater ran out of gas in Greensboro, grabbed an empty gas can and started walking. A bit later he saw an old Vermonter on his porch and afraid to ask for a favor outright, the out-of-stater held up the can and asked, "How long will it take me to walk to the nearest gas station?" No reply came. Thinking the old man might be hard of hearing, the out-of-stater yelled, "How long will it take me to walk to the nearest gas station?" Not a word from the Vermonter. The man yelled his question again but still no response. Annoyed, he stomped off down the road. He'd gone 50 yards when the Vermonter shouted, "About an hour, sonny." "Why didn't you say so before?"

472. A Vermont farmer was picking rocks out of his field with his grandson. The boy asked, "Where'd all these rocks come from, Grandpa?" "The glaciers brought 'em," said the farmer. "Then where'd the glaciers go?"

473. Stranger to farmer beside the road: "Does it matter which road I take to Danville?"

474. Tourist to Vermonter: "How is the best way to get to Grafton from here?"

475. A Texan was once bragging to a Vermonter about how huge his ranch was compared to the Vermonter's little hill farm. "Why my ranch is so big," he said, "I can get in my truck on one side

of the place, drive all day, and still not reach the other side." The Vermonter paused and said . . .

476. Flatlander to Vermonter: "When did the last train leave for Boston?"

477. How many Vermonters does it take to change a light bulb? Four. One to screw it in . . .

478. Stranger to old-time Vermonter: "How's your wife?"

479. Newcomer to Vermonter: "This sure is a beautiful town. Lived here all your life?"

480. Out-of-stater to Vermonter: "What are you going to do when old man Pickens dies?"

481. A traveler, having gotten out of his car, wants to cross a very muddy, rut-filled road. He yells out to a Vermonter sitting on the porch of his house on the other side: "Say, how'd you get over there?"

482. Downstater to Vermonter: "Say, how far is your nearest neighbor?"

483. "Do you suppose it'll ever stop raining?"

484. A talkative lady who was to sit next to President Calvin Coolidge at a dinner party took a wager from a friend that she could not "get three words out of the president all evening." To win the bet she laughingly told Coolidge about the bet at dinner. Solemnly he turned to her and said . . .

485. A lost balloonist from Ohio who drifts out of the clouds over a small Vermont farm shouts down to a Vermonter in his field, "Where the hell am I?"

486. It is said that once when the Connecticut River rose in the spring it changed course and cut a New Hampshire farmer off, leaving his house and entire farm on the west side of the river in Vermont. But the very next spring the river flooded again and returned to its old channel, shifting the farmer back to the New Hampshire side. "Thank God," he said, "I . . ."

487. An undertaker was summoned into the hills of Vermont to a farmer's house that was situated a very long way from town. He was to pick up the body of the dead farmer. Upon his arrival he was met on the porch by the farmer's wife. "He ain't quite dead yet," said she, "but . . ."*

*This one, found in Hale's book, was an original for us.

488. Once during mud season a man was traveling on a back road and came upon a mudhole in which he found a man buried up to his neck. "You're in trouble, ain't you?"he said.**

489. Summer person to Vermonter beside the road: "Say (they always say 'say'), how do you get to Bethel?" Vermonter: "If I were going to Bethel . . ."

490. Newcomer to Vermonter: "That Poultney road sign back at the corner is pointing in the wrong direction, isn't it?"***

491. A visitor to the state once encountered an old Vermonter alongside the road. Seeking to strike up a conversation he said, "I bet you've seen a lot of changes in your lifetime." "Yep," came the terse reply. "And . . ."****

492. We like the way Ralph Nading Hill told this one in the autumn 1950 issue of *Vermont Life*: There was a tourist who "stopped his car on a country road and leaned over the fence to talk with a Vermonter laboring with a hay fork. In the course of the conversation the tourist said, 'You certainly have a lot of characters around here!' Riveting his eyes on the tourist, the Vermonter twanged . . .

**This story was told by Francis Colburn in his famous speech "A Graduation Address." His wording is of course the funniest. Hear in your imagination the *sound* of a heavy Vermont accent as Colburn, perhaps Vermont's most sought-after public speaker of his time, tells the story: "But, boys and girls, to get back to the parable of the muddy road. That year the mud was so deep on the road that my poor old father had to use snowshoes on the road. As he approached the village he seen a hat lying on that muddy road which, as he came nearer, he observed to be moving. In some consternation, he picked up the hat to find the head of his friend and neighbor, Walter Wheeler. 'Walter,' said my father, 'you're in trouble, ain't you?' 'No,' said Walter, 'for I still have my horse under me.'"

***This is quoted directly from Keith Jennison and Neil Rappaport's *Yup . . . Nope and Other Vermont Dialogues* and is our favorite. Jennison's earlier *Vermont Is Where You Find It* is *the* classic book of Vermont humor because it is also very, very wise.

****Along with several others of these stories, this one can be found in Allen R. Foley's *What the Old-Timer Said* (Brattleboro, Vermont: The Stephen Greene Press, 1971). It's an awfully funny book.

CHAPTER 8

Vermont ID's

Every student is familiar with the dreaded ID, that simple little term that says, "Do you know anything about me?" Sometimes they are preceded by the command, "*identify* the following," or "*describe* the following," or "*explain* the significance of the following." We simply say: demonstrate that you could engage in a conversation with a Vermonter when it hinged on an understanding of:

493. Green Mountain Giant
Near the floating island on Sadawga Pond in Whitingham is a 3,400-ton freestanding boulder that is known as the "Green Mountain Giant."

494. Stanchion
A device designed to hold cattle in their stalls (usually for milking purposes). It is V-shaped with the open end on top. When the cow sticks her head through it, one side is quickly closed toward the other and latched. The cow cannot pull her head back out and thus is held securely in place.

495. Mazipskwik
Word for Missisquoi or "place of the flint." It is the main village of the Western Abenaki Tribe.

496. Bear Gram
A unique gift and marketing strategy created by John Sortino consisting of a personalized Vermont Teddy Bear, a card, and a candy treat shipped anywhere in the world.

497. Monadnock

Charles W. Johnson, in his *Nature of Vermont*, defines one as follows: "Monadnocks are large-scale intrusions of younger rock into pre-existing rocks, having squeezed into cracks, pockets, or caverns in a molten state, then solidifying. Most monadnocks are much younger than the host rock into which they have flowed." Mount Ascutney is a monadnock. The more popular meaning is for that of a free-standing or lonely mountain. The Abenaki translation for monadnock is "mountain which sticks up like an island."

498. Horn of the Moon

A road in Washington County, a café in Montpelier, and a pond in East Montpelier. In *Vermont Place-Names*, Esther Swift tells us that "an old Indian is given credit for the picturesque East Montpelier place-name, Horn of the Moon. It seems that once he lost his wife, and later found her at the place he called 'horn of the moon.'"

499. The Potash Kettle

A wonderful publication of the Green Mountain Folklore Society helping to preserve the myths, legends, and traditions of Vermont.

500. Indian Summer

An extended warm spell usually occurring a few days after the first hard frost in autumn.

501. Frost Heaves

Asphalt catapults on paved roads caused by the rising frost in the spring. Bad for drinking coffee while riding in a car.

502. Spigot

Another term for a sap spout.

503. Magic Hat

A microbrewery in South Burlington that brews up beers such as "Hocus Pocus," "Fat Angel," "Miss Bliss," and "Feast of Fools."

504. Phish Food

Chocolate ice cream with marshmallow nougat and caramel swirl and fudge fish, it's a popular flavor of Ben & Jerry's ice cream named for the band *Phish,* who got their start in Burlington. All of the band's proceeds from Phish Food go to environmental efforts for Lake Champlain.

505. Draw-off

When a tie occurs in a livestock pull (horses, ponies, or oxen), a "draw-off" is held to determine the winner. (Also used to refer to the process of drawing-off the syrup from a pan of hot sap.)

506. RO Machine

Reverse osmosis machines are used in water management and purification. They are also used in the maple sugaring process to filter out about 75% of the water from the sap and increase the sugar content before it is boiled down to syrup.

507. Mount Ascutney Train

A pathway of rocks and boulders that originated from Mount Ascutney and were carried from there all the way into Massachusetts by the last glacier. It is said that in the heat of summer in the 19th century, one could hear from atop that mountain in Windsor County the distant angry murmur of what one might call the "Mount Ascutney Curse" echo up from the southern terrain as men and women sweated to remove these rocks from their fields. Today, as we let these open lands revert to brush or build "condo villages" right smack dab in the middle of them—ignoring the incredible human "sunk costs" that went into their creation—perhaps we should listen again for the bygone wail of the "Mount Ascutney Train."

508. Snow Rollers

Nature's snowballs. When a combination of light sticky snow and high winds occurs, the wind actually begins to roll small loops of snow across open fields or down hills. As they roll, they gather size and weight. If conditions are right, snow rollers have been reported in sizes up to 18 inches in diameter.

509. Stone Boat

A flat bed of planks (totalling three to four feet wide and six to ten feet long) with very small rails (two to three inches or so) around the outside onto which stones are rolled. The "stone boat" is then drawn over the ground to a rock pile or stone wall site and tipped over (if the farmer has staged his approach wisely) or unloaded. The front of the boat is curved upward so it will slide easily over rough ground. The stone boat is Vermont's most classic symbol of raw, dusty, sweat-soaked, back-breaking, pebbles-in-your-shoes and grit-on-your-tongue labor. The only way to love a stone boat is to pick stone for a day using a wagon.

510. Ginger Water

Switchel.

511. *The Belle of Brattleboro*

Captain Aaron Betts' cruise boat on the Connecticut River. It's a forty-nine-passenger river boat featuring cruises and charters. On nights when the moon is full, passengers will be treated to ghost stories narrated by a real witch.

512. Moosalamoo

Stretching from the western ridge of the Green Mountains to Lake Dunmore and from Middlebury Gap to Brandon Gap, there are more than 20,000 acres of cliffs, views, waterways, and forests inviting Vermonters and visitors to enjoy the outdoors.

513. Laurentide Ice Sheet

The great glacier that covered Vermont until about 12,000 years ago. It's what caused Vermont's up and downs and back and forths.

514. Ernest Johnson

A black folk singer who traveled through Vermont in the 1940s and 1950s singing songs of African American culture from the South. Mr. Johnson's visits were a welcome event for children of Vermont's rural schools. He charged no fee although the "hat was always passed." He left a generation of Vermont schoolchildren a gift of love, admiration, and joy.

515. Switchel

A cooling drink popular on the farms of Vermont in times past made with various combinations of water and ginger and molasses and vinegar. It is often called "ginger water."

516. Quimby's

This is one of Vermont's most famous resort areas. Located deep in the Northeast Kingdom on Big Averill and Forest Lakes, it is featured in Earle Newton's important history, *The Vermont Story*, as follows: "Up in forest-clad Essex County attractive, red-haired Hortense Quimby now runs [this was written in the late 1940s] the hunting lodge established by her father over fifty years ago. An ardent conservationist and one of the state's best businesswomen, she has developed Quimby's into a family resort, with facilities for the care of children, and guides for the adults who find the wilderness around the Averill lakes a paradise for fishing and hunting." Quimby's is a word synonymous in Vermont with the old-style outdoor resort facility so popular in the first half of the 20th century.

517. The Witch of Wall Street

Hetty Green of Bellows Falls was the richest businesswoman in the world. When she died in 1916 she was worth more than $100 million. According to the Vermont Historical Society's January 1971 issue of *News and Notes*, she "became a familiar figure on the streets of Bellows Falls, Vermont, for the last forty-two years of her life." She married Edward Green of Bellows Falls in 1867. Richard Ketchum of Dorset has written extensively on "The Witch of Wall Street." She was the quintessential penny pincher. The Vermont Historical Society says she was "surely one of the most peculiar figures ever to live in the Green Mountain State."

518. Allemande Left

A maneuver in a square dance. The "gentleman" turns to his left and spins with the "lady" waiting there one full turn. As the turn is completed, the lady is sent back to the left and often the gentleman continues right in a "grand right and left." More difficult to describe in writing than to do, the allemande left is one of those steps that always seems to foul up newcomers to square dancing.

In driving through Vermont, no matter what your purpose or destination, you often see cows grazing on rolling green pastures or huddled around the barn. How well can you identify some of the different breeds such as Line-back, Jersey, Holstein, Guernsey, Dutch Belted, Ayrshire, Hereford, or Durham? Can you name the three we have pictured?

519.

520.

521.

522. Many Vermont farms are now raising non-traditional animals. Can you recognize this creature?

Answers

519. Jersey
520. Scottish Highlander
521. Holstein
522. Alpaca

CHAPTER 9

"Vermont Is a State I Love"*

Familiar Quotations—Yankee Style

In Vermont we are particularly aware of what people say about us. Perhaps that is because we share a unique heritage and live in a land that bespeaks individualism. We have placed legal graffiti in the form of quotes about Vermont on the very walls of the statehouse. We delight in the notions (accurate and inaccurate) that outsiders have about us. Vermonters also have their own literature and their own history. From all this comes our own listing of familiar quotations. Let's see if you're conversant with it.

Fill in the following: (Hint: The spaces provided indicate the number of words in each.)

523. *"Home is a place that when you go there*

_____ _____ _____ _____ _____ _____ ."

(Robert Frost)

524. *"Surrender in the name of the Great Jehovah and*

_____ _____ _____ ."

(Ethan Allen)

525. *"I do not choose to* _____ _____ _____ _____

_____ _____ _____ _____ ."

(Calvin Coolidge)

*Calvin Coolidge said it in 1927. We all feel it.

96

526. *"There is no more Yankee than Polynesian in me but when I go to Vermont, I feel like I am _____ _____ _____ _____ _____ ."*
(Bernard DeVoto)

527. *"Vermonters love the past, but they love _____ _____ _____ _____ ."*
(Dick Snelling)

528. *"The gods of the hills are not _____ _____ _____ _____ _____ ."*
(Ethan Allen)

529. *"_____ _____ _____ _____ _____ and keep the column well closed up."*
(General John Sedgwick)

530. *"You men of northern Vermont . . . living among its rocks and mountains in a region which may be called the _____ of America—you are the people here who have had hearts full of love of freedom which exists in mountain people and who have the indomitable spirit and the unconquerable will which we always associate with the lake and mountain lands."*
(Viscount James Bryce)

531. *"Let us do all we can to keep up the notion among our city cousins that to live 'away up in Vermont' is the American equivalent for being _____ _____ _____ ."*
(Abby Hemenway)

Who said it?

a. George Dewey
b. Stephen Douglas
c. Ira Allen
d. Calvin Coolidge
e. Dick Snelling

f. Tom Salmon
g. George Aiken
h. Prince Otto von Bismarck
i. Sinclair Lewis
j. Theodore Roosevelt
k. William Taft

_____ 532. *"I am glad to hear that so many come to Vermont to spend their money. You should get out of them all you can get."*

_____ 533. *"I love Vermont because of her hills and valleys, her scenery and invigorating climate, but most of all, because of her indomitable people."*

_____ 534. *"The best way to kill something in Vermont is to mandate it."*

_____ 535. *"My idea of a republic is a little state in the north of your great country . . . Vermont."*

_____ 536. *"Vermont is not for sale."*

_____ 537. *"Vermont has always played far more than her part to which she was by population entitled in the affairs of the country."*

_____ 538. *"You may fire when ready, Gridley."*

_____ 539. *"Vermont is the most glorious spot on the face of the globe for a man to be born in, provided he emigrates when he is very young."*

_____ 540. *"I know of no country that abounds in a greater diversity of hill and dale."*

_____ 541. *"I like Vermont because it is quiet, because you have a population that is solid and not driven by the American mania—that mania which considers a town of 4,000 twice as good as a town of 2,000."*

_____ 542. *"Either impeach him or get off his back."*

Who said the following of whom?

543. *"I am but one in fifty-five million; still in the opinion of this one fifty-five-millionth of the country's population, it would be hard to better President _____'s administration."*
    a. George Aiken about Herbert Hoover's administration.
    b. Mrs. Calvin Coolidge about Calvin Coolidge's administration.
    c. Mark Twain about Chester Arthur's administration.
    d. James Garfield about Chester Arthur's administration.

To whom did each refer?

544. Walter Prescott Webb said the following of whom?

    He "broke his health and brought himself to the grave prematurely by the intensity of his inactivity."

545. George Washington said the following of whom?

    "There is an original something in him that commands attention."

546. Sen. Jacob Collamer, President Lincoln's confidant, said of which Vermont town?

    "The good people of _____ have less incentive than others to yearn for heaven."

Who said the following?

    "The New Hampshire Grants in particular, a country unpeopled and almost unknown in the last war, now abounds in the most active and most rebellious race on the continent and hangs like a gathering storm on my left."

    (547.) General _____

548. What did Ethan Allen say when he demanded the surrender of Fort Ticonderoga?

a. *"Surrender or I shall lay this fort as low as Sodom and Gomorrah."*

b. *"My apologies for the disruption; may I have your sword, sir?"*

c. *"Put on your pants and show us where you keep the rum."*

d. None of the above (as far as we know).

During the Vietnam War, a Vermont politician gave the president some advice on the war that received national attention and, in fact, was pretty much followed.

549. The politician was _____.

550. His advice was to _____.

Answers
Familiar Quotations

523. "Home is a place that when you go there *they have to take you in.*"
524. "Surrender in the name of the Great Jehovah and *the Continental Congress.*"
525. "I do not choose to *run for President in nineteen hundred and twenty-eight.*"
526. "There is no more Yankee than Polynesian in me but when I go to Vermont I feel like I am *traveling towards my own place.*"
527. "Vermonters love the past, but they love *the future far more.*"
528. "The gods of the hills are not *the gods of the valleys.*"
529. *"Put the Vermonters in front* and keep the column well closed up." This command was issued at the Battle of Gettysburg. Also at the Battle of Gettysburg, General Doubleday, watching the Second Vermont Brigade, shouted "Glory to God, glory to God, see the Vermonters go at it." During the Civil War it was Dixie's General Stonewall Jackson who was credited with the swiftest marches and greatest endurance. But the Vermonters proved his equal. The First Vermont marched 32 miles in a night and a day to reach Gettysburg on July 2nd. The Second Vermont Brigade marched 132 miles in six days in sweltering southern July heat to reach the battle July 1st.
530. *Switzerland*
531. "Let us do all we can to keep up the notion among our city cousins that to live 'away up in Vermont' is the American equivalent for being *exiled to Siberia.*"
532. k. William Taft
533. d. Calvin Coolidge
534. e. Dick Snelling
535. h. Prince Otto von Bismarck
536. f. Tom Salmon
537. j. Theodore Roosevelt
538. a. George Dewey

539. b. Stephen Douglas. In one of the great quirks of U.S. electoral history, Stephen Douglas, a native Vermonter, was defeated four-to-one in Vermont when he ran for president against a flatlander from Illinois named Abe Lincoln. Vermonters, it seems, were more interested in issues like slavery than birthright.

540. c. Ira Allen

541. i. Sinclair Lewis

542. g. George Aiken (referring to Richard Nixon).

543. c. Mark Twain about President Arthur. Garfield might have said it, but if he did it wasn't to anyone on the planet since the reason Arthur was president was because Garfield had been shot dead.

544. Calvin Coolidge

545. Ethan Allen

546. Woodstock

547. John Burgoyne

548. d. But we do know they did consume most of the fort's rum. Historian B. A. Botkin writes that one Israel Harris, who was present, passed on to his ancestors what he believed to be Ethan Allen's real words: "Come out of there, you goddam old rat." Most people like to believe he really did say "Surrender in the name of the Great Jehovah and the Continental Congress."

549. George Aiken

550. "Declare victory and leave." Judson Hale says this about the Aiken quote: "It's somehow comforting to Americans when a Vermonter acts like 'a Vermonter.' We all smiled and felt good inside when Aiken advised President Lyndon Johnson to declare the Vietnam War won and pull out the troops. It would not have been as amusing or even as wise if someone from another state had said it."

CHAPTER 10

Footprints on Granite

Vermont History

"Contrary Country" is what Ralph Nading Hill calls it. And it was. In an earlier book we described Vermont's view of Vermont's history as follows: "At war with New York, shooting it out with the British, negotiating with Canada, storming Congress to demand admittance into the Union, playing Robin Hood with Albany sheriffs, capturing the largest British fort in America even before the Revolutionary War had begun . . . that is Vermont as Vermonters see it. The exploits continue . . . many true, some myth, all of them feeding a healthy state ego." Accepted truth is to historians what bee trees are to bears—they like to tear them down. But the "accepted truths" of Vermont's past endure like the mountains in which they were born. Indeed, one of the most accurate of the "accepted truths" about Vermont is that we have one of the best cadres of state historians in North America. They are shepherded in part by the Vermont Historical Society, which is one reason only the truest of the truths remain true: all of them are subject to the incessant bombardment of good ol' Yankee squint-eyed critique. If you score poorly on this chapter, membership in the Vermont Historical Society is your clearest route to redemption.

551. In 1979 Winooski city officials considered a plan for the city to help conserve energy. The plan called for

    a. building a dam on the Winooski River.
    b. enforcing a 10 P.M. curfew.
    c. putting a dome over the city.
    d. mandating carpooling.

552. William Keough, former Superintendent of Burlington Schools, was also known for

    a. his early support for the voucher system.
    b. being one of the hostages in Iran in 1981.
    c. his marksmanship.
    d. winning the World Series of Poker in 1978.

553. When Samuel de Champlain conducted his famous battle with the Indians, he fought on the side of the Algonquins against the

    a. Mohawks.
    b. Penobscots.
    c. Mohegans.
    d. Iroquois.

554. What were the Green Mountain Boys organized to do?

555. The first governor of Vermont was

    a. Thomas Chittenden.
    b. Ira Allen.
    c. Jacob Bayley.
    d. Ethan Allen.

556. Charles Dawes, vice-president to Calvin Coolidge, was the only vice-president to

    a. die while in office.
    b. be awarded the Nobel Peace Prize.
    c. resign.
    d. be born in the same state as the president he served under.

557. The first female governor of Vermont was

    a. Lola Aiken.
    b. Fanny Allen.
    c. Lillian Proctor.
    d. Madeleine Kunin.

558. What did George Van Dyke and Dan Bosse have in common and why are they key figures in the history of Vermont?

559. Vermont's 200-year-old "Blue Laws" which required Sunday store closings were held unconstitutional by the Vermont Supreme Court in

a. 1902.
b. 1936.
c. 1964.
d. 1982.

560. Who of the following was not a Green Mountain Boy?

a. Seth Warner
b. Remember Baker
c. Jacob Bayley
d. Ira Allen

561. Matthew Lyon was elected to Congress from four different states.

a. True
b. False

562. On July 7, 1984, this accident killed five people and injured about 150 in Chittenden County:

a. a chain reaction 60-car pileup in the early morning fog on I-89.
b. a Boston-bound airliner skidded into a parking lot at Burlington International Airport.
c. Amtrak's Montrealer jumped the tracks after a heavy rain.
d. excited fans at a rock concert at Burlington's Municipal Auditorium got out of hand and charged the stage.

563. In the 1960s Vermonters were shocked when someone fired at a black minister's home in the Northeast Kingdom. This event became known as _____.

564. A town in Vermont was originally named Wildersburgh. At town meeting, a vote on the substitute names of Holden and _____ ended in a tie. Champions were picked to defend each name. Fisticuffs ensued and a victorious blacksmith won the town the current name of

a. Montpelier.
b. Barre.
c. Bristol.
d. Ludlow.

565. In 1974 President Gerald Ford came to Vermont to

a. inspect damage from a freak flood that caused more damage than any flood in Vermont since 1927.
b. honor Senator George Aiken on his retirement from the U.S. Senate.
c. vacation at the Woodstock Inn.
d. speak in Bennington on Bennington Battle Day.

566. The only Revolutionary War battle fought entirely on Vermont soil was the Battle of

a. Bennington.
b. Hubbardton.
c. St. Albans.
d. Strafford.

567. "Earth People's Park" was located in

a. Plainfield.
b. Marlboro.
c. Norton.
d. Island Pond.

568. On January 15, 1777, Vermont signed a Declaration of Independence from New York at

a. Windsor.
b. Westminster.
c. Hubbardton.
d. Dorset.

569. In the 1800s the Georgia Legislature suggested that Irish laborers be hired to dig a ditch around Vermont and float the state out to sea. Why?

    a. Because Vermont favored abolition of slavery.

    b. Because Vermont, following Maine's lead, prohibited liquor.

    c. Because Vermont opposed formation of the Mason-Dixon Line.

    d. None of the above.

570. What did Vermonters Charles Paine, Erastus Fairbanks, J. Gregory Smith, and John Page all have in common besides the fact that they all served as governors of the state?

571. Which of the following happened in 1978?

    a. Vermont's statewide lottery began.

    b. Windham College in Putney closed.

    c. neither a nor b

    d. both a and b

572. What was Vermont's first name (two words)?

573. Adopted in 1779, the Vermont State Motto is

    a. Liberty and Freedom.

    b. Freedom and Unity.

    c. Liberty and Unity.

    d. Liberty, liberty, liberty, liberty . . . liberty.

574. The first white settlement in Vermont was located in

    a. Brattleboro.

    b. Vernon.

    c. Isle La Motte.

    d. Shaftsbury.

Match the event with the correct year from the time line.

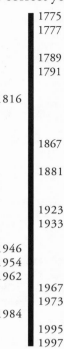

1775
1777

1789
1791

1816

1867

1881

1923
1933

1946
1954
1962
1967
1973
1984
1995
1997

575. _____ The year of no summer.
576. _____ The last panther was shot.
577. _____ Vermont's first TV station went on the air.
578. _____ Vermont joined the Union.
579. _____ The first Democrat since the Civil War was elected governor.
580. _____ The Republic of Vermont was formed.
581. _____ The Westminster "Massacre" occurred.
582. _____ *Vermont Life* was established.
583. _____ A beverage container deposit law was enacted.
584. _____ The Island Pond Raid was carried out.
585. _____ Vermont ETV went on the air.
586. _____ The first state gasoline tax was adopted.
587. _____ Ethan Allen died.
588. _____ Vermont passed its first child-labor law.
589. _____ Act 60 Education Act was passed.
590. _____ Calvin Coolidge died.
591. _____ The first Wal-Mart opened in Vermont.

592. In 1960 an 86-year-old man, whom Vermonters will always credit as one of their own, read a poem to the nation in Washington, D.C. entitled "The Gift Outright." Who was he?*

Which of the following were *not* true when:

593. Calvin Coolidge was president.

   a. Vermont sent two representatives to Congress along with its two senators.
   b. Red clover was the state flower.
   c. The state was losing population.

594. Philip Hoff was governor.

   a. I-91 was not completed.
   b. The Yankee Nuclear Power Plant in Vernon was under construction.
   c. Act 250 was in effect.

595. Ira Allen was alive.

   a. The Vermont State Senate was in operation.
   b. Montpelier was the state capital.
   c. The state's population was less than 100,000.

596. During the Civil War, Vermonters (commanded by Gen. George J. Stannard of St. Albans) were credited with making one of the most decisive and significant military maneuvers of the war. What was it?

The (597.) _____ Tavern, headquarters of the Green Mountain Boys, is located in (598.) _____.

597. a. Flowing Bowl   598. a. Bennington
     b. King George   b. Killington
     c. Catamount   c. Shaftsbury
     d. Killington   d. Panton

*Actually he didn't read it. He was blinded by the bright sun and had to recite it by heart.

109

599. Ethan Allen was captured by the British in the Revolutionary War and spent nearly three years in captivity.

a. True
b. False

600. In 1953 the Rutland railroad

a. adopted diesel engines for the first time.
b. eliminated passenger service completely.
c. shut down its commuter train (named the Wallingford Flyer) due to a lack of passengers.
d. became the first train in the U.S. to provide headphones (radio) for its passengers.

601. Lumber from the forests of Vermont went into the ships that fought in1776 at the decisive battle of Valcour Island, which delayed the British from attacking Fort Ticonderoga. Historian Earle Newton says of this event, in *The Vermont Story*, "from the virgin forests of Vermont this stubborn, energetic leader had constructed a navy of his own." This leader was

a. Ethan Allen.
b. Ira Allen.
c. Benedict Arnold.
d. Seth Warner.

602. In February 1943, a Vermonter named George Fox

a. flew with the American forces who delivered the first bombing raid on the Japanese homeland.
b. became one of the "Four Immortal Chaplains" who went down with his ship in the North Atlantic.
c. became Chief of Staff to General George Patton in his African campaign.
d. became the first American to lead a tank attack against the Third Reich.

603. Identify: Captive Johnson

The New Hampshire colonial governor who"granted" the land for over 125 towns in Vermont was named Benning (604.) _____. The first town he granted was (605.) _____. The intention was to make each town a square of (606.) ____ miles on a side. The charters provided town lots for schools, the Church of England, the first settled minister, and (607.)_____.

604.	605.	606.	607.
a. Allen	a. Norwich	a. one	a. a landfill dump
b. Bailey	b. Bennington	b. six	b. a fort
c. Wentworth	c. Dummerston	c. twenty	c. an industrial park
d. Hubbard	d. Hubbardton	d. thirty	d. himself

608. One of the state's leading employers, IBM, moved into Vermont in

    a. 1947.
    b. 1957.
    c. 1967.
    d. 1977.

609. Vermont's last legal execution (by the electric chair) took place in what year?

    a. 1938
    b. 1954
    c. 1963

610. He was the most famous scout and Indian fighter of the last and most decisive of the French and Indian Wars. His exploits included the incredible raid on the St. Francis Indians in 1759. He became a true legend on the northern frontier. He is called by Ralph Nading Hill a "bulwark of the frontier." Says Hill, "there has never been a more fearless scout and Indian fighter." His name was?

611. In 1997, 1.2 million acres were farmed in Vermont. In 1920 _____ were.

    a. 2.4 million
    b. 4.2 million
    c. 10.6 million
    d. 20.4 million

612. When was the Tunbridge Fair first held?

    a. 1867
    b. 1901
    c. 1948
    d. 1888

613. A huge thunderstorm had a major influence on why this building is in this book. What is the building and why was the thunderstorm so important?

Answers
Vermont History

551. c. putting a dome over the city.
552. b. being one of the hostages in Iran in 1981.
553. d. Iroquois. (Vermont was known on ancient maps as "Iroquoisia.")
554. Drive out the Yorkers.
555. a. Thomas Chittenden.
556. b. be awarded the Nobel Peace Prize.
557. d. Madeleine Kunin.
558. They were both great lumbermen of the north country. Van Dyke was in truth a New Hampshire man, although he was born in Quebec. But his father was born in Highgate. He rose from nothing and became the "most potent force the whole length of the Connecticut" according to Robert E. Pike, whose *Tall Trees, Tough Men* will prickle the spine of anyone who has spent time in the woods with saw and team and anyone else with enough sense to believe there was a time when guts, endurance, and the capacity to accept pain were a part of everyday life. Van Dyke operated a saw mill at McIndoe Falls and built the Upper Coos Railroad of Vermont. For years he ran his lumber company from Bloomfield, Vermont. When he died at a Connecticut River drive at Turner's Falls in 1902, he was a multimillionaire. Dan Bosse was called by Pike the "greatest riverman in the north country." He left his job with the Brown Paper Company to participate in the last great drive on the Connecticut in 1915, which consisted of 500 rivermen who floated 65 million feet of logs down the river the full length of Vermont's eastern border and beyond.
559. d. 1982.
560. c. Jacob Bayley
561. b. False. It was only *three* different states: Vermont, Kentucky, and Arkansas, which was still a territory.
562. c. Amtrak's Montrealer jumped the tracks in Williston, Vermont, after a heavy rain.

563. the Irasburg Affair
564. b. Barre.
565. b. honor Senator George Aiken on his retirement from the U.S. Senate.
566. b. Hubbardton.
567. c. Norton.
568. b. Westminster.
569. a. Because Vermont favored abolition of slavery.
570. They all served as presidents of railroads. (Paine headed the Vermont Central Railroad; Fairbanks, the Connecticut and Passumpsic Railroad; Smith, the Vermont and Canada Railroad; and Page, the Rutland Railroad.)
571. d. both a and b
572. New Connecticut
573. b. Freedom and Unity.
574. c. Isle La Motte. Although Fort Dummer in the town of Brattleboro was the first *permanent* white settlement in Vermont, the first white settlement was established in 1666 by Captain Pierre La Motte. The French tore it down about ten years later.
575. 1816
576. 1881
577. 1954
578. 1791
579. 1962, Phil Hoff
580. 1777
581. 1775
582. 1946
583. 1973
584. 1984
585. 1967
586. 1923
587. 1789, at age fifty-four.
588. 1867
589. 1997
590. 1933
591. 1995

592. Robert Frost
593. c. The state was losing population.
594. c. Act 250 was in effect.
595. a. The Vermont State Senate was in operation.
596. At the most decisive moment in the most decisive phase of the most decisive battle in the Civil War (the Battle of Gettysburg), Stannard flanked the charging Confederates under General Pickett. The Vermont Historical Society calls it this way in the September 1972 issue of *News and Notes*: "When the Confederate forces began to group for the charge on Cemetery Ridge, they formed two lines that somehow became separated and had to regroup while moving up the slope of Cemetery Ridge in front of the two Vermont brigades. Stannard's bugles sounded as he wheeled his troops to attack the Confederates on their right flank. The surprise was decisive: The Confederates broke in disorder and surrendered by the hundreds."
597. c. Catamount
598. a. Bennington
599. a. True
600. b. eliminated passenger service completely.
601. c. Benedict Arnold.
602. b. became one of the "Four Immortal Chaplains."
603. Captive Johnson was the daughter of Mrs. Suzanne Johnson, born on the trail after an Indian raid on Deerfield, Massachusetts. Earle Newton places the town of birth as Cavendish. She spent the first few years of her life in various Indian camps, prisons, the households of the French in Canada, and a boat between North America and England. Her mother, according to Ralph Nading Hill in *Yankee Kingdom*, lived a life of incredible hardship but survived to report:
    "My daughter, Captive, still keeps the dress she appeared in when brought to my bedside by the French nurse at the hospital; and often refreshes my memory with the past scenes, when showing it to her children . . ..
    "My aged mother, before her death, could say to me, arise daughter and go to thy daughter, for thy daughter's daugh-

ter has got a daughter; a command which few mothers can make and be obeyed."

604. c. Wentworth
605. b. Bennington
606. b. six
607. d. himself
608. b. 1957.
609. b. In 1954 Donald Demag and Francis Blair were executed in Windsor for killing a Springfield woman after an escape from prison.
610. Robert Rogers. It is difficult for those reared in the ease and comfort of post-war America to truly understand the raw magnitude of the suffering endured and the courage displayed by men like Robert Rogers. Reading Ralph Nading Hill helps, however. One of the editors of this volume was given *The Winooski: Heartway of Vermont* early in life by his Aunt Polly and then later *Yankee Kingom*. It still brings goose bumps when Hill recalls with us, for instance, Whittier's lines about Robert Rogers:

> Robert Rawlin!—Frosts were falling
> When the Ranger's horn was calling
> Through the woods to Canada . . .

611. b. 4.2 million
612. a. 1867. It is one of the oldest town fairs in the U.S.
613. The Constitution House in Windsor. The framers of the Vermont Constitution were about to abandon their task and rush off to fight the British when a thunderstorm struck and kept them inside to finish their work.

CHAPTER 11

Believe It or Not

Vermont is such a unique state that it often defies categorization on many aspects of Americana. Because it is so different, many people have trouble deciphering fact from fiction and myth from reality. Which of the statements below do you think are believable?

I Believe It   I Don't Believe It

614. Almost 2,000 Vermonters showed up to the casting call for a Jim Carrey movie being made in Vermont. _____ _____

615. Three U.S. Presidents died on the 4th of July, but only Vermonter Calvin Coolidge was born on the 4th of July. _____ _____

616. The boulders placed strategically along Burlington's Church Street Marketplace for decorative purposes were imported from New Hampshire. _____ _____

617. Five out of Vermont's last six governors were born outside Vermont. _____ _____

618. There is no commercial bungee jumping anywhere in Vermont. _____ _____

619. In 1878, seventeen deer were imported from New York State because we'd run out of them in Vermont.

620. The Shelburne Museum is actually located in the town of Charlotte.

621. Comedian Jerry Seinfield is married to a UVM graduate who also graduated from Burlington High School.

622. Mt. Philo in Chittenden County was once an island.

623. There are more cows than people in Vermont.

624. In 1896 the bones of a great white shark were uncovered in a swamp near Lake Dunmore.

625. The mountains of the Northeast Kingdom are really New Hampshire's White Mountains.

626. Ethan Allen was not born in the United States.

627. In 1973 the remains of a three-thousand-year-old Indian culture were found during excavations in Swanton.

628. As late as 1965, towns like Victory (population 46) and Stratton (population 38) each sent one legislator to the House of Representatives in Montpelier, while towns like Rutland (population 12,000) and Burlington (population 38,000) sent only one also.   _____   _____

629. When the Green Mountain Boys were formed as a regiment in the Revolutionary War, Ethan Allen was not chosen to lead them.   _____   _____

630. In 1849 the bones uncovered in a railroad bed excavation near Charlotte were found to be those of a whale.   _____   _____

631. Montpelier has the smallest population of any capital city of the 50 states.   _____   _____

632. In 1968 it cost George Aiken $4.28 to run for reelection to the U.S. Senate.   _____   _____

633. Burlington was the first Vermont town or city ever to elect a socialist mayor.   _____   _____

634. No state lost a greater percentage of its sons in the Civil War than Vermont.   _____   _____

635. The Sheldon Museum is actually located in Middlebury.   _____   _____

636. When visiting Burlington, actor Harrison Ford ordered more than five "Stoli on the rocks" at Nectar's.   _____   _____

637. "Moonlight in Vermont" is the Vermont State Song.   _____   _____

638. Danville, Vermont, is the headquarters for the American Society of Dowsers.   _____   _____

639. Calvin Coolidge grew up, died, and was buried in Vermont but did not carry his home town in the presidential election of 1924.   _____   _____

640. Explorer Jacques Cartier was the first white man to look upon the land that became Vermont.   _____   _____

641. "Hail Vermont" is the Vermont State Song.   _____   _____

642. The first quadruple homicide recorded in Vermont happened in Belvidere in 2001.   _____   _____

643. Alex Aldrich, executive director of Vermont Arts Council, was the first Vermonter to win a cool million on TV's *Who Wants to be a Millionaire?*   _____   _____

644. "These Green Mountains" is the Vermont State Song.   _____   _____

645. The Vermont State Flower, the red clover, is not indigenous to Vermont and was imported from England.   _____   _____

646. The official Vermont State Nut is the butternut.   _____   _____

647. As of the 2000 census, no state had a smaller population than Vermont.   _____   _____

648. The *New York Times,* the *New York Tribune*, and the *New York Daily News* (the nation's largest daily for years) were all founded by Vermonters.   _____   _____

649. Vermont Royster, former editor of the *Wall Street Journal‚* was born in Vermont.   _____   _____

650. Vermont high-school students score higher on SAT's than the national average.   _____   _____

651. Calvin Coolidge's first name was really John.   _____   _____

652. Vermont has never executed a woman.   _____   _____

653. When ordering horses and oxen around, you often hear the words "gee" and "haw." "Gee" means left and "haw" means right.   _____   _____

654. It takes 40 gallons of sap to make one gallon of maple syrup.   _____   _____

121

655. Vermont has one American Indian-operated casino.

656. The band *Phish* gave their first live performance at the Burlington High School Prom in 1983.

657. The nation's first interstate welcome center opened in Guilford beside I-91.

658. The number of murder convictions in Vermont in 1970 was four. In 1997 it was also four.

659. On March 5–6, 2001, Burlington accumulated 23 inches of snow and St. Johnsbury accumulated 6 inches.

660. The state of Vermont has a dozen daily newspapers.

661. The oldest writers' conference in the country is the Middlebury College Bread Loaf Writers' Conference.

Answers
Believe it or Not

614. False. Over 3,000 showed up.
615. True.
616. False.
617. True. Howard Dean was born in New York, Dick Snelling in Pennsylvania, Madeleine Kunin in Switzerland, Thomas Salmon in Ohio, and Philip Hoff in Massachusetts. Only Deane Davis was a Vermonter.
618. True.
619. True.
620. False. If it were, it would be called the Charlotte Museum.
621. True.
622. True.
623. False. People outnumber cows about 2-to-1.
624. False. You've seen too many movies!
625. True.
626. True. Ethan Allen was born in the British colony that later became the American state of Connecticut.
627. True.
628. True.
629. True. Seth Warner was elected instead.
630. True.
631. True.
632. False. It was a much greater amount—$17.09.
633. False. Barre had a socialist mayor in 1912.
634. True.
635. Of course—any fool knows that!
636. True.
637. False.
638. True.
639. False. Silent Cal carried Plymouth 165-7 for 96% of the two-party vote. (The Progressives got one vote.) Statewide he received 83%.
640. False. It was Samuel de Champlain in 1609.

641. False.
642. False. A couple and their two children were found shot to death in Essex in 1945.
643. False. He only won $125,000.
644. True. "Hail, Vermont" was adopted in 1938, but in 1999 a contest was held for a new state song. "These Green Mountains" composed by Diane B. Martin and arranged by Rita Buglass Gluck won.
645. True.
646. False. Vermont has no state nut.
647. False. Wyoming was lower.
648. True. You should believe this one. Horace Greeley from Poultney founded the *Tribune*, George Jones, also from Poultney, was co-founder of the *Times*, and William Field of Rutland founded the *Daily News*.
649. False. Vermont historian Charles Morrissey reported in 1978 that he knew of no Vermonter named "Vermont." The only person he had ever discovered with the first name "Vermont" was Vermont Royster, but he was born and raised in North Carolina. Morrissey, in an article entitled "Names from Vermont History" (*Vermont Life's Annual Guide*, 1978), also reports David Ludlum's discovery of a beauty of a Vermont name—a minister in Bridport named Increase Graves.
650. False. Vermont students averaged 1017, three points below the national average.
651. True.
652. False. We hanged two.
653. False. "Gee" means *right* and "haw" means *left*.
654. True.
655. False. There are no casinos in Vermont.
656. False. Their first live performance was at a ROTC Halloween dance in a UVM cafeteria.
657. True.
658. True.
659. True.
660. False. There are only 9.
661. True.

THE WEATHER PAGES

They say that Vermonters are a taciturn lot, hard to talk to and not quick to strike up a conversation. Perhaps that is because, while most Americans talk about the weather to start off conversations, in Vermont we find that subject too depressing. Actually, Vermont's weather is okay. It wears on you, true. Yet despite some messy exceptions we are spared the massive disasters that befall people in other states. One thing especially nice about Vermont's weather is David Ludlum's treasure of a book about it called *The Vermont Weather Book*, which provides the documentation for much of the following:

662. The worst winter storm of the year, the "Crown of Winter Storms," often occurs in the month of March. In recent years the worst of these occurred in March of

    a. 2001.
    b. 1999.
    c. 1997.
    d. 1994.

663. The foggiest month in the Connecticut River Valley is the month of

    a. April.
    b. June.
    c. September.
    d. February.

664. The coldest temperature recorded in Vermont was in Bloomfield in 1933 when it was

    a. -75°.
    b. -50°.
    c. -40°.
    d. so cold that a fire in a woodlot froze solid at 8:15 A.M. on February 1.

665. Vernon holds the record for the highest temperature in Vermont. In 1911 the temperature there rose to

   a. 98°.
   b. 105°.
   c. 110°.
   d. 112°.

666. _____ are used to determine a relative value for heat consumption and costs.

667. When it reached its deepest point, how deep was the snow on top of Mount Mansfield during the winter of 2000–01?

   a. 5 feet
   b. 7 feet
   c. 11 feet
   d. 14 feet

668. Deane Davis was the only governor to declare Vermont a "disaster area" because of a snowfall.

   a. True
   b. False

669. Vermonters who have lived here since 1977 can already brag that they have lived through

   a. the coldest Christmas Day.
   b. the 2nd coldest February.
   c. the 4th and 5th coldest Januaries recorded in Vermont in the last 100 years.
   d. all of the above.

670. In _____ Vermont experienced the most severe hurricane of the 20th century.

   a. 1912
   b. 1938
   c. 1950
   d. 1977

The following is a series of 5 questions. Pick the correct answer from the list below.

a. April
b. August
c. December
d. February

e. January
f. July
g. November
h. September

Question	Month
671. The coldest month of the year is	_____
672. The wettest month of the year is	_____
673. The warmest month of the year is	_____
674. The driest month of the year is	_____
675. The month of the year with the temperature closest to the yearly average is	_____

676. Vermonters share a fatalism about the weather. They get nervous when it's nice in the winter and keep looking apprehensively at the heavens knowing that sometime soon they'll "pay" for it. According to David Ludlum, the greatest debt paid in the 20th century occurred in Bennington on _____ 14, 1943, when the temperature _____ overnight.

a. January / fell 72°, from +60 to −12
b. January / fell 70°, from +40 to −30
c. February / fell 77°, from +45 to −32
d. December / fell 70°, from +35 to −35

677. "Lake effect" means it is colder in the fall near a big lake.

a. True
b. False

678. The record for deepest snow on Mount Mansfield was set in which year?

a. 2001
b. 1996
c. 1969
d. 1948

679. On the darkest day of the year, we get about _____ fewer hours of sunlight in Vermont than on the brightest day of the year.

a. 2.5
b. 4.5
c. 6.5
d. 8.5

680. The worst weather in Vermont's history occurred in 1816. We call this year "eighteen hundred and _____ _____ _____."

681. In 1954 Vermont was visited by a hurricane (or hurricanes) named

a. Carol.
b. Edna.
c. Hazel.
d. All of the above.

682. The state has experienced many floods but the most devastating and costly one in the last century was the Great Flood of

a. 1895.
b. 1927.
c. 1952.
d. 1976.

683. How many people died in the Great Flood referred to in question 682?

    a. 6
    b. 29
    c. 94
    d. 200

684. When people in Burlington were celebrating New Year's Day 1966, the warmest temperature that day was

    a. 45°.
    b. 56°.
    c. 64°.
    d. 72°.

685. According to the official records, it has never been 70° anywhere in Vermont in February.

    a. True
    b. False

686. In the month of September in Vermont the highest temperature ever recorded was _____ and the lowest temperature was _____.

    a. 90 / 25
    b. 95 / 20
    c. 100 / 15
    d. 105 / 10

Answers
The Weather Pages

662. a. 2001.
663. c. September.
664. b. -50.
665. b. 105.
666. Degree days. According to Ludlum, "Degree days are based on the premise that artificial heating is not needed at mean temperatures above 65° F and are calculated by taking the mean temperature, that is, half the sum of the day's maximum and minimum temperatures, and subtracting the mean from the base of 65."
667. c. 11 feet (132 inches)
668. b. False. Davis did it in 1969, and Howard Dean also declared Vermont a disaster area due to the March 2001 snow storm.
669. d. all of the above.
670. b. 1938. If you answered c, you were close. In November 1950, a huge windstorm did almost as much damage as in 1938. It was not an authentic hurricane since it did not originate over a tropical sea and did not have the true characteristics of a hurricane.
671. e. January
672. b. August
673. f. July
674. d. February
675. a. April. T. S. Eliot was right, "April is the cruelest month."
676. c. February, the temperature fell 77°, from +45 to –32
677. b. False.
678. c. 1969 (149 inches; in 1996 it reached135 inches)
679. c. 6.5
680. "eighteen hundred and *froze to death*."
681. d. Carol came in August, Edna in September, and Hazel in October.
682. b. 1927. Montpelier also experienced a doozy in 1992 when floating ice jammed up the Winooski River.

683. c. 94 people died, which is the highest toll from a natural disaster in the state's history.
684. b. 56°. It set a record for the Queen City.
685. a. True. But it did reach 70° in January in Dorset in 1950.
686. c. Both Vernon and Bellows Falls recorded 100° in 1953 in September and back in 1947 Dorset dropped to 15°.

CHAPTER 12

Those Who Labor in the Earth

"Those who labor in the earth," said Thomas Jefferson, "are the chosen people of God." Vermonters know that's an exaggeration—of sorts. Vermont without farmers could be a good place too, but it could never be Vermont; and while there are lots of good places, there is only one Vermont. Ever since Vermont began, those who worked the land have defined our every contour—the economy, the politics, the villages and towns, indeed the very landscape that enwraps our lives. We know them by their sounds and sights and smells—the distant "chomp and grind" of a baler on a quiet June afternoon, a herd of cattle steaming in a barnyard yellow with the cold sun of January, the smell of fresh manure and new cut hay: signs of life and rebirth, of labor and accomplishment. The chosen people of God? Maybe not. But close. Very close.

687. Of the following Charles Mraz of Middlebury was best
known for his

  a. revolutionary cider press.
  b. bee venom treatments.
  c. prize-winning bulls.
  d. ability to milk goats.

688. On average, which cow listed below is the largest at maturity?

  a. Holstein
  b. Jersey
  c. Guernsey
  d. Hereford

689. The national headquarters of the world's largest dairy cattle breeding association is located in Vermont. Where?

a. Addison
b. Cabot
c. Brattleboro
d. Bradford

690. What do William Asack of Barton, Mary Lou Schmidt of Dummerston, and David Howe of Tunbridge all have in common?

a. They raise rabbits for meat.
b. They produce honey.
c. They grow and sell Christmas trees.
d. They create web pages for Vermont dairy farms.

691. During which of the following decades did Vermont lose the greatest number of farms?

a. 1900–1910
b. 1940–1950
c. 1970–1980
d. 1990–2000

692. In 1998 Paul Casey of Hinesburg started a non-traditional farm by raising

a. fallow deer.
b. elk.
c. moose.
d. rodeo bulls.

693. Which kind of cow is the most popular among Vermont's dairy farmers?

a. Holstein
b. Jersey
c. Guernsey
d. Ayrshire

694. Vermont produces fewer pounds of milk per day now than it did in 1950.

    a. True
    b. False

695. Who is the Vermont Commissioner of Agriculture?

    a. Leon Graves
    b. Fred Tuttle
    c. David Wolk
    d. Elizabeth Ready

696. How many farms were there in Vermont according to the 2001 U.S. Census of Agriculture?

    a. 587
    b. 2,630
    c. 6,800
    d. 10,670

697. What do the following people have in common: Rich Paquette, Todd Hardie, Ben Davis, Bill Mares, and George Willy?

    a. They raise rabbits for meat.
    b. They produce honey.
    c. They grow and sell Christmas trees.
    d. They create web pages for Vermont dairy farms.

698. You are talking to two Vermonters, one from, say, Bridport and the other from, say, Norwich. In answer to the question, "Where do Vermonters milk their cows?" one says, "in the 'bahn'"; the other says, "in the 'barrn.'" Which one says 'bahn'?

    a. The one from Bridport
    b. The one from Norwich

699. Vermont is America's largest producer of maple syrup.

    a. True
    b. False

700. With dairy farming threatened, many Vermonters are raising other kinds of critters. If you plan to raise deer, the fence posts you use to keep them in must be at least _____ feet high.

    a. 6
    b. 9
    c. 12

701. The Olallie Farm in South Newfane sells only

    a. organic vegetables.
    b. free-range chicken eggs.
    c. fresh turkeys.
    d. daylilies.

702. Vermont is number one in New England in total milk production.

    a. True
    b. False

703. To help Vermont businesses lure customers at holiday time, Wilson's Farm in Putney will provide

    a. live reindeer.
    b. on-site horse-drawn sleighs.
    c. lambs dressed as Santa's elves.
    d. fully decorated Christmas trees.

704. In a single year, Vermont farmers induce Vermont cows to produce

    a. over 2.5 million pounds of milk.
    b. over 200 million pounds of milk.
    c. over 2.5 billion pounds of milk.

705. Jessica is the name of a famous Vermont

    a. horse.
    b. cow.
    c. moose.
    d. pig.

706. In 1840 there were 291,948 people in Vermont. How many sheep were there?

    a. 108,766
    b. 291,948
    c. 552,900
    d. 1,681,814

707. Something is perched on top of the *V* in the Vermont Seal of Quality label. What is it?

    a. A cow
    b. An apple
    c. A cow eating an apple
    d. A red clover

The top three dairy producing counties in New England are found in Vermont. Name them.

708. _____

709. _____

710. _____

711. In 2000, Vermont chickens produced enough eggs to provide one egg per day for everyone in the state.

    a. True
    b. False

712. About what percentage of Vermont's land area is being actively farmed?

    a. 6%
    b. 20%
    c. 31%
    d. 54%

713. Vermont's highest apple-producing county is

    a. Grand Isle.
    b. Addison.
    c. Bennington.
    d. Windham.

Agri-ID's

Identify each of the following:

714. The Bay State Cow Path
The "Bay State Cow Path," running from Middlebury to Brattleboro, covered much of what is now Route 30. It was a route followed by Boston buyers wanting fresh meat for the Boston market.

715. PTO
With apologies to parents and teachers, PTO also stands for *Power Take Off*, a device that radically changed the character of mechanized farm work in Vermont. "Hooking it up to the PTO" saved an awful lot of work. Located at the rear of a tractor, it allows the farmer to run machinery (often hauled behind the tractor) with power from the tractor itself—power that operates mowers, rakes, and so on. Running the baler off the PTO is much easier than off an engine perched on the baler (or what have you) itself.

716. Merry Mulch
A program started by the Vermont Department of Agriculture in 1988 to prevent holiday trees from ending up in landfills. It later became a model for other states and countries.

717. Rowen
Rowen is the second cutting of hay from a field. Since it grows slower than the "first cutting," it gathers more protein. Rowen is therefore more highly valued as feed. We like the description Richard Ketchum (of Blair and Ketchum's *Country Journal*) uses in the introduction to his (highly recommended) book of essays, *Second Cutting*: "You can't expect the same quantity the second time around, but you have a shot at putting up hay that is more tender and nutritious, with a high protein content and quality that won't deteriorate during the winter."

718. Bag Balm
This ointment, made in Lyndonville, Vermont, is used for cows' udders. However, soon its soothing properties were discovered to be

useful for humans too, and it became a standard item on the shelf above the sink where the milking-machines are washed. It is applied to almost anything that hurts, chafes, or itches in and around the barn.

719. The Extension Service and Agricultural Experiment Station at the University of Vermont provides which publications free of charge to the general public?

    a. *Procedures for Improving Udder Health*
    b. *Dry Cow Therapy*
    c. *Teat Dipping Facts*
    d. All of the above

720. The Brown Swiss is a breed of

    a. goat.
    b. sheep.
    c. cow.
    d. goose.

721. Which breed of cattle is used for oxen?

    a. Holstein
    b. Ayrshires
    c. Charolais
    d. All of the above

722. Which kind of cow gives milk with the higher butterfat content, Holsteins or Jerseys?

When you wonder if your neighbor's pig has had her young yet, you ask: Has she *pigged?* What about

723. rabbits? _____
724. sheep? _____
725. cows? _____
726. goats? _____

727. On September 26, 1908, Edward Moote of Weathersfield accomplished a tremendous feat.

    a. He milked 32 cows in an hour.
    b. He cut, split, and piled 5 cord of 4-foot wood in a day.
    c. With his team of Durhams, he plowed 32 acres in a day.
    d. He debeaked 4,200 chickens in a day.

728. There is a prohibition on spreading manure between December 15 and April 1.

    a. True
    b. False

The Maple Corner

729. How many years does it take to grow a tree big enough to tap?

    a. 20
    b. 40

730. What is the minimum size a tree should be before it's tapped?

    a. 6 inches in diameter
    b. 10 inches in diameter
    c. 15 inches in diameter

731. Throughout the 1990s and into the 21st century, Vermont has out-produced its closest competitor (New York) in syrup production by about _____.

    a. 10%
    b. 50%
    c. 100%

732. A tree 22 inches in diameter will support 3 taps.
    a. True
    b. False

733. Vermont's leading county in maple syrup production is

    a. Bennington.
    b. Franklin.
    c. Windsor.
    d. Caledonia.

734. To produce enough sap to make one gallon of maple syrup, you need about

    a. 2–3 taps.
    b. 4–5 taps.
    c. 7–8 taps.
    d. 10–11 taps.

735. Maple sugaring season usually lasts

    a. 2–3 weeks.
    b. 4–6 weeks.
    c. 4 months.
    d. all year.

736. According to the official standards for the state of Vermont, "pure maple syrup which is free of any materials other than pure, clear, clean liquid maple syrup . . . and has a light transmittance between the range of 60.4% Tc to 44.0% Tc" is considered

    a. Fancy Grade.
    b. Grade A Medium Amber.
    c. Grade A Dark Amber.
    d. Grade B.

Can you identify the farm machinery pictured on the next page?

737.

738.

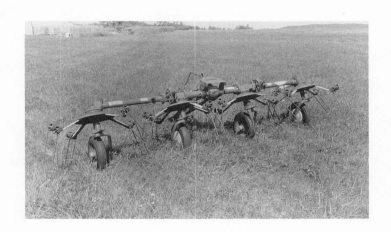

739.

Answers
Those Who Labor in the Earth

687. b. bee venom treatments. He was the pioneer of this therapy and thousands visited him in Middlebury for treatment before he died in 1999 at the age of 94. He wrote *Health and the Honeybee* and for over 60 years maintained New England's largest apiary.

688. a. Holstein. They usually weigh about 1,500 pounds.

689. c. Brattleboro. The breed is the Holstein.

690. c. They grow and sell Christmas trees.

691. b. 1940–1950. In that decade we lost 4,539 farms—more than one a day. In the last decade of the 20th century we lost about 300.

692. b. elk.

693. a. Holsteins. They give an average of 6.4 gallons of milk per day.

694. b. False

695. a. Leon Graves

696. c. 6,800, of which 1,783 were dairy farms.

697. b. They produce honey. Bill Mares' honey touts the motto *Bee Happy in Your Work.*

698. b. The one from Norwich

699. a. True, accounting for just over 37% of the nation's entire maple syrup output.

700. a. 6

701. d. daylilies.

702. a. True

703. a. live reindeer, which they will rent or lease.

704. c. over 2.5 billion pounds of milk.

705. b. cow, and in 1986 in Shrewsbury, she had a love affair with an unnamed moose.

706. d. 1,681,814 (about 6 per person).

707. d. A red clover

708. Addison

709. Franklin

710. Orleans
711. b. False. About 156 million eggs short.
712. b. 20%. In 1920 it was 73%. Think about that.
713. b. Addison.
714–18. Agri-ID's. Answers are with the questions.
719. d. All of the above. You can also get *Raising Pigs for Home Use*, *Fish Farming in Vermont*, and *Talking About Turkey* among many others.
720. c. cow.
721. d. All of the above
722. Jerseys. Jersey owners refer to Holstein milk as "chalk and water." Holstein owners seldom dispute this but claim they have forgotten the insult by the time they reach the bank.
723. kindled
724. lambed
725. calved
726. kidded
727. b. By 4:15 P.M., he was done. Moote (50 years and 150 pounds) added another one-eighth of a cord for "good measure" and then, to the cheers of the crowd, he collected $100 for his task and was placed atop the pile for pictures. Over $5,000 in bets had been laid. Among the losers was the journalist Samuel G. Blithe. What interesting things you can read about as a member of the Vermont Historical Society!
728. a. True
729. b. 40
730. b. 10 inches in diameter
731. b. 50%
732. a. True
733. b. Franklin.
734. b. 4–5 taps.
735. b. 4–6 weeks.
736. c. Grade A Dark Amber.
737. baler
738. hay rake
739. manure spreader

THE TOWN MEETING PAGES

740. Only one town in Vermont elects people to attend town meeting from its neighborhoods. Which is it?

741. In the early 1980s Vermont received prolonged national and international attention for its town meeting votes requesting

   a. the two Germanys be reunited.
   b. a treaty to prevent global warming.
   c. a nuclear weapons test ban treaty.
   d. that Vermont be permitted to join Quebec as part of a new nation.

742. On average, in towns of under 2,500 population about _____ of a town's registered voters will be in attendance at town meeting.

   a. 10%
   b. 20%
   c. 45%
   d. 60%

743. In a Vermont town, the list of items to be resolved at a town meeting is called the _____.

744. How many registered voters at a town meeting does it take to call for a paper (secret) ballot?

745. If you want to have an issue placed on the formal list of items to be resolved at town meeting, you may do so by having ____ of the voters sign a petition supporting you.

   a. 5%
   b. 10%
   c. 15%
   d. 20%

746. You are at a traditional Vermont town meeting. There is an election for a town office. The result is Jones-60, Smith-50, and Brown-40. What happens next?

    a. Jones is declared the winner.
    b. Smith goes home mad.
    c. There is another election between Jones, Smith, and Brown.
    d. The second choices on Brown's ballots are distributed between Jones and Smith.
    e. a and b

747. In 1936 on town meeting day, Vermonters voted "No" (30,795 "for" and 42,873 "against") to a proposed public works project for the state. What was it?

748. Town meetings are held in Vermont on which of the following?

    a. Monday night or Tuesday Day
    b. Monday night, Saturday Day, or Tuesday Day
    c. Tuesday Day or Tuesday Night
    d. Any of the times listed above

749. The "Quorum" at a Vermont town meeting is

    a. 5% of registered voters in attendance.
    b. 5% of eligible voters in attendance.
    c. 10% of registered voters in attendance.
    d. There is no specified percentage of citizens needed to conduct a town meeting.

750. A Vermont town may vote to disallow any non-citizen of a town from speaking at a town meeting including the governor or the president of the United States.

    a. True
    b. False

751. Road commissioners are

    a. always elected at town meeting.
    b. always appointed by the selectpersons.
    c. elected unless a vote is taken to have the selectpersons appoint.
    d. appointed by the selectpersons unless the town votes to elect.

752. In towns of under 2,500 population, about _____ of those present at a town meeting are apt to participate verbally (not counting the seconding of a motion) at least once.

    a. 20%
    b. 40%
    c. 55%
    d. 65%

753. Charles Kuralt of CBS's *On the Road* and *Sunday Morning* fame was once asked what his favorite place in all America was. He said he found it in _____, Vermont, on town meeting day.

754. Who once said that town meeting was "the wisest invention ever devised by the wit of man for the perfect exercise of self-government"?

    a. Ethan Allen
    b. Richard Snelling
    c. Thomas Jefferson
    d. Madeleine Kunin

755. When you vote for town officers or on other town matters on a previously prepared paper ballot throughout town meeting day, instead of during the meeting, you are voting by _____ ballot.

756. How many voters does it take to suspend the rules at a town meeting? _____

757. In 1974 the town of _____, Vermont, made national news by becoming the first government in America to request the impeachment of Richard Nixon.

758. How many amendments may be offered to a proposal on the floor at the same time?

   a. 1
   b. 2
   c. 3
   d. As many as the voters damn well please.

759. In the late 1980's Governor Madeleine Kunin was seen standing in a light-falling snow in the parking lot outside the Duxbury town meeting. She was:

   a. waiting for her car to be "jumped."
   b. waiting for her state police driver to get back from a diner in Waterbury.
   c. waiting for the town meeting to finish voting on whether or not she should be allowed to speak.
   d. waiting for TV cameras to arrive from Channel 3 to tape her appearance at the meeting.

760. Town meeting attendance is generally lower at night meetings than at day meetings.

   a. True
   b. False

Answers
Town Meeting Pages

740. Brattleboro
741. c. a nuclear weapons test ban treaty
742. b. 20%
743. warning
744. seven
745. a. 5%
746. c. But if no one gets a majority after three ballots, the moderator drops the lowest vote-getter from the race.
747. The Green Mountain Parkway proposal, which envisioned building a highway running along the spine of the Green Mountains.
748. d. any of the times listed
749. d. There is no specified percentage of citizens needed.
750. a. True
751. d. appointed by the selectpersons unless the town votes to elect.
752. b. 40%
753. Strafford
754. c. Thomas Jefferson
755. Australian
756. two-thirds
757. Thetford
758. b. 2
759. c. waiting for the vote on whether she should be allowed to speak.
760. a. True

CHAPTER 13

Under the River and through the Woods

Vermont Hunting and Fishing

While skiing is Vermont's high-publicity sport, there is an entire strata of Vermont's society that knows outdoor sports in another way. They know the sharp, chest-tightening cry of a blue jay in November hardwoods at dawn, or the urgent snap and tug as their night crawler disappears under a log in the dark swirl of a mountain brook agush with the waters of spring. These are the people who are called by an ancestral longing to reunite with the wild. There are those who point (perhaps rightly) to the unreality of it. But the feeling is real, and it helps sustain Vermont's most ardent environmentalists—the outdoor sportspeople. The following are questions from their world.

761. The first time permits were issued to hunt moose in the 20th century occurred in

    a. 1949.

    b. 1968.

    c. 1986.

    d. 1993.

762. The legal brook trout limit in Vermont is

    a. 0.

    b. 5.

    c. 12.

    d. There is no limit.

763. Vermont is the top turkey hunting state in New England.

    a. True

    b. False

764. The recommended clothing color to wear while hunting with firearms is called

    a. "Green Mountain Red."

    b. "Forest Bright."

    c. "Hunter Orange."

    d. "Camouflage Red."

765. It is illegal to hunt bear with dogs in Vermont.

    a. True

    b. False

766. No fishing license is required for ice fishing.

    a. True

    b. False

767. A person may shoot a black bear at any time in defense of his property.

    a. True

    b. False

768. The record lake trout taken in Vermont was an even 34 pounds caught in 1981 in Lake

    a. Willoughby.

    b. Champlain.

    c. Morey.

    d. Dunmore.

769. To be allowed to fish in all parts of the Connecticut River, you need

    a. a Vermont Resident Fishing License.

    b. a New Hampshire Resident Fishing License.

    c. both a and b.

    d. either a or b.

770. Within 20 pounds, give the weight of the biggest buck entered in the Vermont Big Game Trophy Program.

771. The Vermont Fish and Wildlife Department considers the wild turkey to be "Big Game."

    a. True
    b. False

772. A hunter cannot shoot a swimming deer.

    a. True
    b. False

773. How many deer were taken in the 2000 season in Burlington?

774. For fishing, the legal day begins at

    a. sunrise.
    b. midnight.
    c. 6 A.M.
    d. one half hour before sunrise.

775. Scientifically, it's known as *Meleagris gallopavo silvestris*. The head is naked and a chalky blue. The male has spurs on his legs. What is it?

776. The Fish and Wildlife's BOW Program held in Craftsbury refers to

    a. "Becoming an Outdoor Woman."
    b. teaching youngsters how to use bow and arrows.
    c. "Basics of Wildlife."
    d. "Beware of Wildlife."

777. As a landowner, you may not ask a hunter to leave your land unless you have posted "No Trespassing" signs.

    a. True
    b. False

778. When ice fishing in Lake Champlain, you are allowed to use _____ lines at a time.

   a. 2
   b. 15
   c. 30
   d. any number of

779. It is permissible to shoot and keep a 50-pound doe in Vermont's bow and arrow deer season.

   a. True
   b. False

Can you identify the county where in 2000:

_____ 780.   The most wild turkeys were killed?

_____ 781.   The most deer were killed?

_____ 782.   The fewest deer were killed?

_____ 783.   The heaviest bear on Vermont's all-time trophy list was shot?

_____ 784.   The heaviest deer on Vermont's all-time trophy list was shot?

785. It's deer season. You shoot a deer legally. Now you must report it. And you must do so within

   a. 1 hour.
   b. 8 hours.
   c. 24 hours.
   d. 48 hours.

786. There is a federal fine of $100,000 for killing an eastern mountain lion in Vermont.

   a. True
   b. False

787. Measured in total pounds taken, which fish is the most important food fish in Vermont?

 a. Brook Trout
 b. Walleyed Pike
 c. Yellow Perch
 d. Smelt

788. In 1990 a new state record brown trout was taken by Barry Bouker of Whitingham on the Sherman Reservoir. It weighed

 a. 10 pounds 6 ounces.
 b. 18 pounds 4 ounces.
 c. 22 pounds 3 ounces.

The following are weights of all-time record fish taken in Vermont through 2000. Match the weight with the fish caught.

789. _____ Chain Pickerel   a. 2 pounds 2 ounces.

790. _____ Northern Pike   b. 10 pounds 4 ounces.

791. _____ Yellow Perch   c. 6 pounds 4 ounces.

792. _____ Largemouth Bass d. 30 pounds 8 ounces.

793. _____ Tiger Muskie   e. 17 pounds 13 ounces.

794. The first closed season on white-tailed deer (from January 10 to June 10) was established in the year 1825.

 a. True
 b. False

795. In the late 1700s in Bennington it was voted that for "any _____ that is killed in Bennington, the person shall be paid two coppers, the person bringing in the tail."

 a. bobcat
 b. rattlesnake
 c. panther
 d. wolf

796. The bounty on porcupine was dropped in

    a. 1994.
    b. 1974.
    c. 1954.
    d. 1934.

797. In Manchester, Vermont, there is something that should appeal to Vermonters interested in fishing. What is it?

    a. A fly fishing museum
    b. A fish hatchery
    c. A manufacturer of specially designed fishing canoes
    d. The largest stuffed horn pout in existence

798. There is no limit on the number of _____ you may trap in a single season in Vermont.

    a. otters
    b. mink
    c. muskrats
    d. all of the above

799. If you are using a Rhode Island Red Hackle, you are

    a. hunting wild geese.
    b. crow hunting.
    c. trout fishing for brookies.
    d. calling wild turkeys.

800. In the Fish and Wildlife Department's list of trophy gobblers the heaviest bird shot was by Richard Gamache. He got it in Alburg and it weighed

    a. 22.75 lbs.
    b. 19.5 lbs.
    c. 18.812 lbs.
    d. 26.2 lbs.

801. If you bag one deer (buck or doe) in bow and arrow or in the traditional "gun" season, you may not shoot a buck during Vermont's muzzleloader deer season.

    a. True
    b. False

802. The spring limit for wild turkeys is

    a. 1 turkey.
    b. 2 bearded turkeys, usually males.
    c. 3 turkeys, bearded or not.
    d. there is no spring season for turkey.

803. The black bear population in Vermont is estimated at

    a. 1,000–1,500.
    b. 2,500–3,000.
    c. 3,000–3,500.
    d. 4,500–5,000.

Answers
Hunting and Fishing

761. d. 1993.
762. c. 12.
763. a. True, although there are a lot of turkeys in New Hampshire.
764. c. "Hunter Orange."
765. b. False
766. b. False
767. a. True, as long as the game warden is notified.
768. a. Lake Willoughby. The trout was caught by a New Hampshire man, John Staples.
769. d. Either will work, but a nonresident license is not valid beyond the low water mark on the Vermont side of the river.
770. 269 pounds, recorded by Ernest Gaskin.
771. a. True
772. a. True, although they might make an exception if it's swimming in your outdoor Jacuzzi.
773. 0
774. b. midnight.
775. The wild turkey.
776. a. "Becoming an Outdoor Woman." This program brings women together in Craftsbury for survival skills, fly fishing, kayaking, hunter safety and much, much more.
777. b. A landowner can demand a person leave the land whether it is posted or not.
778. b. 15 lines (2 hooks per line allowed)
779. a. True. There is no limit on the size of deer taken. Shooting fawns is permissible, though highly unlikely since deer have their young in the early spring.
780. Rutland—755
781. Rutland—2,849
782. Grand Isle—380
783. Essex—514 pounds

784. Essex—269 pounds
785. d. 48 hours, and you must go to a "deer-reporting station" to do so.
786. a. True, plus a $2,000 fine to the state.
787. c. Yellow Perch
788. c. 22 pounds 3 ounces.
789. c. Chain Pickerel—6 pounds 4 ounces.
790. d. Northern Pike—30 pounds 8 ounces. (Bernard Golob got it at Glenn Lake.)
791. a. Yellow Perch—2 pounds 2 ounces.
792. b. Largemouth Bass—10 pounds 4 ounces.
793. e. Tiger Muskie—17 pounds 13 ounces.
794. b. False. It was established in 1779.
795. b. rattlesnake. Charlotte McCartney reported in the *Vermont History News* that farms in neighboring Windsor County "were so infested [with rattlesnakes] until the turn of the century that many hired men walked off their jobs."
796. c. 1954.
797. a. The Museum of American Fly Fishing
798. d. all of the above
799. c. trout fishing for brookies.
800. a. 22.75 lbs.
801. b. False. You can. "A person shall not take more than three deer in a calendar year."
802. b. 2 bearded turkeys, usually males.
803. c. 3,000–3,500.

CHAPTER 14

Rocky Vermont

Why do folks live in the hills? Why do they persist in clinging to steep, rocky slopes and in living under conditions which modern humanitarianism says can only produce unhappiness for them, when some of them, at least, have the means to move out and go elsewhere and go in debt all over just like other folks? The reason is that some folks just naturally love the mountains, and like to live up among them where freedom of thought and action is logical and inherent.

George Aiken

Realtors in Vermont will tell you the key questions people ask before buying property here are: Is there a fireplace? And, Is there a view of the mountains? In a sense our Green Mountains are a metaphor for the Vermont dilemma of the 21st century: Do people want Vermont to be a place to look at, or to live with? We have argued elsewhere that "Rural means living with the earth. It means understanding a few things well. It means knowing a few people completely. It means patience with nature. It means, most of all *involvement* with the planet. One lives in the country to *be with* the mountains, not look at them." How to be with our mountains in a human way and not sully them or detract from their majesty—a condition that is absolutely secure only when they are alone and apart from us. That is our challenge.

804. In what town is the highest point in Vermont?

　　a. Stowe
　　b. Underhill
　　c. Morristown
　　d. Sherburne

Match the trail with the mountain:

_____ 805. Brownsville Trail   a. Mt. Roosevelt
_____ 806. Burr & Burton Trail   b. Mt. Hunger
_____ 807. Clark Brook Trail   c. Mount Equinox
_____ 808. Jerusalem Trail   d. Mt. Ascutney
_____ 809. Waterbury Trail   e. Mt. Ellen

810. Which of the following counties has the most acres of Green Mountain National Forest?

a. Addison
b. Bennington
c. Rutland
d. Windham

811. There's a scary-sounding mountain in Goshen called

a. Scary Mountain.
b. Haunted Mountain.
c. Skeleton Mountain.
d. Horrid Mountain.

812. Camel's Hump has also been known as

a. Camel Mountain.
b. The Couching Lion.
c. Mount Camel.
d. The Sleeping Camel.

813. You are hiking the Long Trail. Which peak won't you cross?

a. Ascutney
b. Pico
c. Jay
d. Camel's Hump

814. In Addison County, there is a mountain named for poet _____ _____.

Match the slogan with the ski area:

_____ 815. "Mountains of Adventure"　a. Mt. Snow
_____ 816. "Wild in Nature"　b. Ascutney
_____ 817. "Mountain for All Seasons"　c. Mad River Glen
_____ 818. "Endless Adventures"　d. Smuggler's Notch
_____ 819. "Ski It If You Can"　e. Killington
_____ 820. "The Coolest Mountain.　f. Bromley
　　　　　The Warmest Memories"

821. The name "Vermont" means

　　a. an ever-green mountain.
　　b. green mountains.
　　c. a mountain of maggots.
　　d. no one is certain.

822. What percent of Vermont's total land area is consumed in the Green Mountain National Forests?

　　a. 1%
　　b. 5%
　　c. 10%
　　d. 20%

823. Prominent parts of Mount Mansfield are known as

　　a. the Father, the Child, the Mother.
　　b. the Forehead, the Nose, the Chin.
　　c. the House, the Woodpile, the Shed.
　　d. the Peak, the Summit, the Ridge.

824. Which of the following is *not* a mountain in Vermont?

　　a. Blue Ridge Mountain
　　b. Salt Ash Mountain
　　c. Mount Jefferson
　　d. Mother Myrick Mountain

825. The Union High School in Bristol is named after a mountain. Which one?

    a. Union Mountain
    b. Mt. Anthony
    c. Mt. Abraham
    d. Shaker Mountain

826. How long is the Long Trail (not counting the side trails)?

    a. 63 miles
    b. 163 miles
    c. 263 miles
    d. 463 miles

827. Stratton Mountain is located in which part of the state?

    a. North
    b. South
    c. East
    d. West

828. Hoosac Mountain is in which county?

    a. Windham
    b. Bennington
    c. Washington
    d. Rutland

Match the ski area with the town in which it's located:

_____	829.	College Snow Bowl	a. Woodstock
_____	830.	Cochran's Ski Area	b. Richmond
_____	831.	Suicide Six	c. Middlebury

832. The scenic rock profiles at Smugglers' Notch are known as

    a. the Hunter and His Dog.
    b. the Smuggler and His Treasure.
    c. Man and Indian.
    d. the Old Man in the Mountain.

833. The northeastern corner of Vermont is called

    a. the Northeastern Highlands.
    b. the Granite Hills.
    c. the Northeast Kingdom.
    d. all of the above.

834. He lived on a farm on Camel's Hump in Duxbury. The _____ Skyline Trail is named after him. He constructed the last 48 miles of the Long Trail himself. His name is _____ .

835. Which mountain doesn't fit?

    a. Mount Mansfield
    b. Camel's Hump
    c. Pico Peak
    d. Mount Equinox

836. The Green Mountain Club was founded in

    a. 1860.
    b. 1910.
    c. 1932.
    d. 1948.

Everyone knows about Danby marble and Barre granite. Match these other towns with the material found in the mountains there.

_____ 837. Strafford	a. asbestos
_____ 838. Hyde Park	b. gold
_____ 839. Poultney	c. copper
_____ 840. Plymouth	d. slate

841. In Salisbury there is a cave named for

    a. Thomas Chittenden.
    b. Ethan Allen.
    c. Seth Warner.
    d. Vincent Naramore.

842. The Indian name for this mountain is "Long View in All Directions." The mountain is?

a. Burke Mountain
b. Mount Mansfield
c. Jay Peak
d. Glastonbury Mountain

843. This mountain's name is formed from two Indian words meaning "the place where the top is." The name of the mountain is?

a. Camel's Hump
b. Mount Equinox
c. Hogback Mountain
d. Mt. Ascutney

844. He founded the Green Mountain Club and the Long Trail. His life, according to Vrest Orton in 1950, was "one of the most selfless and most useful lives of any public figure in Vermont." He once drew attention by suggesting (as a member of the Vermont Academy faculty in Saxtons River) that no boy should be allowed to graduate from a Vermont high school until he had climbed at least one Vermont mountain. Edward Crane, who edited the *Burlington Free Press*, said of him:

"In him were combined the vision
Of a prophet
The determination of a full day
And the driving force of a battering ram.
He believed in the power of ideas!"

His name was _____.

Match the resort with the mountain:

_____ 845. Killington Resort   a. Mount Snow
_____ 846. Grand Summit Resort   b. Mount Mansfield
_____ 847. Stowe Mountain Resort   c. Pico Mountain

848. Many of Vermont's principal mountains share the same name. Of the following names, which is the most popular?

    a. Bald
    b. Bear
    c. Green
    d. Spruce
    e. White Rocks

849. Of the following mountains which is the highest?

    a. Killington
    b. Mt. Ellen
    c. Jay Peak
    d. Ascutney

850. What is called the "Grand Canyon of New England"?

    a. Huntington Gorge
    b. Quechee Gorge
    c. Devil's Gulch in Eden
    d. East Putney Falls and Pot Holes

Identify these distinctive mountains in Vermont.

851.

852.

Answers
Rocky Vermont

804. b. Underhill. Mansfield's Chin is 4,397 feet. The Nose in Stowe is only 4,020.
805. d. Brownsville Trail—Mt. Ascutney
806. c. Burr & Burton Trail—Mount Equinox
807. a. Clark Brook Trail—Mt. Roosevelt
808. e. Jerusalem Trail—Mt. Ellen
809. b. Waterbury Trail—Mt. Hunger
810. b. Bennington with 123,503 acres
811. d. Horrid Mountain.
812. b. The Couching Lion.
813. a. Ascutney
814. Robert Frost
815. d. "Mountains of Adventure"—Smuggler's Notch
816. a. "Wild in Nature"—Mt. Snow
817. b. "Mountain for All Seasons"—Ascutney
818. e. "Endless Adventures"—Killington
819. c. "Ski It If You Can"—Mad River Glen
820. f. "The Coolest Mountain. The Warmest Memories"—Bromley
821. d. One story is that the Rev. Samuel Peters named the state Verd Mont from atop Mount Pisgah. Charlie Morrissey, a well-known "Vermontist," writes "Peters . . . insisted that he named the state Verd Mont, for Green Mountain, not Vermont, which translates from the French as 'Mountain of Maggots.' Piqued at his critics he curtly observed: 'If the former spelling is to give way to the latter, it will prove that the state had rather be considered a mountain of worms than an ever green mountain.'"
822. b. 5%
823. b. the Forehead, the Nose, the Chin.
824. c. Mount Jefferson is in New Hampshire; all the others are mountains that are in Vermont.
825. c. Mt. Abraham
826. c. 263 miles

827. b. South (flatlanders might also say west)
828. b. Bennington
829. c. College Snow Bowl is in Middlebury.
830. b. Cochran's Ski Area is in Richmond.
831. a. Suicide Six is in Woodstock.
832. a. the Hunter and His Dog.
833. d. all of the above.
834. Monroe / Will S. Monroe
835. d. Mount Equinox is not in the Green Mountains. It is in the Taconic mountain range.
836. b. 1910. All Vermonters should give thanks for the Green Mountain Club. It has quietly and without fanfare or strident politics protected our great treasure. It maintains hundreds of miles of footpaths in Vermont.
837. c. Strafford—copper
838. a. Hyde Park—asbestos
839. d. Poultney—slate
840. b. Plymouth—gold
841. b. Ethan Allen.
842. a. Burke Mountain
843. b. Mount Equinox, from the Indian words Agwanok Ewanok.
844. James P. Taylor
845. c. Killington Resort at Pico Mountain
846. a. Grand Summit Resort at Mount Snow
847. b. Stowe Mountain Resort at Mount Mansfield
848. a. There are six mountains in Vermont, all over two thousand feet, named Bald. (There are also six named Burnt.) There are seven that have the name "Little" such as Little Equinox and Little Wilcox Peak. There are five Spruce, four White Rocks, three Green, and two Bear.
849. a. Killington at 4,235 feet (Mt. Ellen, 4,083; Jay Peak, 3,861; Ascutney, 3,144)
850. b. Quechee Gorge
851. Camels Hump
852. Jay Peak

THE 1990s PAGES

Here are the "stories of the year for the 1990s." Put them in chronological order.

853. _____ a. A January ice storm downs trees and power lines and thousands lose power, some for as long as 10 days.

854. _____ b. State Supreme Court ruling gives the okay to civil unions but delays implementation so the legislature can determine how.

855. _____ c. Republican Governor Richard Snelling dies suddenly at home and Lt. Gov. Howard Dean takes the office.

856. _____ d. Recession beginning in December of 1989 continues to affect Vermonters well into this year.

857. _____ e. Faced with $44 million deficit, Governor Dean institutes a series of budget cuts.

858. _____ f. State Supreme Court finds the school financing system to be unconstitutional.

859. _____ g. Socialist Bernie Sanders defeats incumbent congressman, Republican Peter Smith.

860. _____ h. Ice jams in the Winooski River in March flood downtown Montpelier.

861. _____ i. Lt. Gov. Barbara Snelling suffers a stroke and abandons race for governor.

862. _____ j. Long-time Speaker of the House Ralph Wright is denied reelection.

863. Which of the following did *not* occur in the 1990s?

a. Tambrands Inc. closes in Rutland.
b. "Act 200" passes the legislature.
c. "Ben" of Ben & Jerry's turns the company over to Robert Holland, Jr.
d. Vermont gets its first Wal-Mart.

864. In the 1990s Bill Clinton visited Vermont and had lunch at a famous Burlington diner. It is called

a. The Parkway.
b. Libby's Blue Line Diner.
c. Henry's Diner.
d. The Oasis.

865. In the 1990s Vermont broke the state's single-year record for bankruptcies.

a. True
b. False

866. In 1994 Alexander Solzhenitsyn left the town of _____ , where he had been living in seclusion, and returned to his native land of Russia.

a. Castleton
b. Cabot
c. Cavendish
d. Corinth

867. In 1999 Vermont lost a poet of whom novelist Howard Frank Mosher once said, "If _____ wasn't a genius, he was as close to one as any one I have ever known." He lived in Orleans and wrote 500 poems about village life in Vermont. He was _____.

868. In 1991 David Budbill published a series of poems originally developed as theater performances. It was called "_____: The Complete Poems."

869. In the 1990s the Vermont population surpassed _____ for the first time in its history.

a. 600,000
b. 700,000
c. 900,000
d. 1,000,000

870. In 1992 a Vermont-based band released its first work on a major label called "A Picture of Nectar." The band is named _____.

871. In the 1990s there were more people of Black or African American ancestry than people of Asian ancestry living in Vermont.

    a. True
    b. False

872. When 79-year old Fred Tuttle ran for the Senate, what was his slogan? _____ _____

873. In 1996 Alexander and Imogen Miller made the national news when _____ was found in their rundown farmhouse in East Orange, Vermont.

    a. an original copy of the Moscow Covenant
    b. several skeletons related to prehistoric catamounts
    c. a photograph of Abraham Lincoln signing the pardon for Vermont's "sleeping sentinel"
    d. $3 million worth of antique cars, gold, and other treasures

874. In 1994 a controversial dam on the _____ River owned by Citizens Utilities was washed away by high water. Environmentalists and trout fishermen cheered.

    a. Winooski
    b. West
    c. Clyde
    d. Lamoille

875. Jeffrey Nichols, a resident of the Chittenden County town of Charlotte, earned fame in 1994 for

    a. being the first man to swim Lake Champlain in November (Burlington to Port Kent).
    b. selling a dairy cow worth $7,500,000.
    c. allegedly being the worst deadbeat dad in the nation.
    d. sighting a catamount on Mt. Philo.

Answers
The 1990s Pages

853. g.
854. c.
855. h.
856. d.
857. j.
858. e.
859. i.
860. f.
861. a.
862. b.
863. b. "Act 200" passes the legislature.
864. d. The Oasis.
865. a. True
866. c. Cavendish
867. James Hayford
868. Judevine
869. a. 600,000
870. Phish
871. b. False
872. Spread Fred
873. d. $3 million worth of antique cars, gold and other treasures. For definition and reference of the Moscow Covenant noted in answer *a*, see Frank Bryan and Bill Mares, *Out! The Vermont Secession Book*.
874. c. Clyde
875. c. allegedly being the worst deadbeat dad in the nation.

CHAPTER 15

A Modest Anarchism

Vermont Politics

If there is one thing for which Vermont is known nationally, it is its politics. Trouble is, most of what is known is wrong! We used to be known as conservative. True, we were Republican to the very core until the early 1950s. But we have never been conservative. Poor, perhaps, but never conservative. Now some people say Vermont is the most liberal state in the nation. Yet people who insist on using the word "most" to modify words like "liberal" or "conservative" to modify "Vermont" display a fundamental ignorance of the state. We like the words of Paul Goodman, who described our politics as "a modest anarchism and plenty of decentralization," or Bill Schubart, who, lamenting the loss of the native Vermonter to author Annie Proulx, called our politics "innately humanistic and radical."

876. The most Democratic municipality in Vermont in the 2000 Presidential election was

    a. Winooski.
    b. Norwich.
    c. Burlington.
    d. Marlboro.

877. Vermont's first primary election was held in which year?

    a. 1870
    b. 1916
    c. 1932
    d. 1952

878. 1902 was a critical year in Vermont politics. In that year

  a. the legislature voted to extend the term of governor from one year to two.
  b. the House of Representatives was reduced in size from 286 members to 246.
  c. a statewide referendum to allow localities to sell alcoholic beverages was passed.
  d. the "Bull Moose Progressives" elected their candidate governor of Vermont.

879. Of the last 20 gubernatorial elections held in Vermont (1962-2000) how many were won by a candidate living in Chittenden County?

  a. 8
  b. 11
  c. 14
  d. 16

880. When was the last time a governor was elected who lived in one of Vermont's six northern counties?

  a. 1936
  b. 1952
  c. 1960
  d. 1972

881. Which of the following politicians has lost the most statewide general election races in Vermont?

  a. John McClaughry
  b. Bernie Sanders
  c. Jan Bakus
  d. Peter Diamondstone

882. Vermont passed its first law relating to campaign finances in

  a. 1816.
  b. 1902.
  c. 1952.
  d. 1972.

883. The Vermont Supreme Court's decision that led to Act 60 is known as

    a. The Dooley Decision.
    b. The Brigham Decision.
    c. The Ginsberg Decision.
    d. The Confusing Decision.

Match the Senator with the county they represent:

884. _____	Thomas Bahre	a. Windsor
885. _____	Nancy Chard	b. Orleans
886. _____	Vincent Illuzzi	c. Addison
887. _____	Richard McCormack	d. Windham

888. Which Vermont county was strongest for Ross Perot in 1992?

    a. Windham
    b. Bennington
    c. Essex
    d. Addison

889. Who was the last incumbent governor to be defeated in a general election for reelection?

890. If no candidate in the general election for governor receives a majority of the popular vote, then

    a. the candidate with the most votes is declared elected.
    b. a runoff election is held in 6 weeks time between the 2 leading candidates.
    c. a joint assembly of the Vermont House and Senate decides the matter by a plurality vote.
    d. the Vermont Senate decides the matter by a plurality vote.

891. Moderate Democrats in the Vermont House of Representatives have been referred to as:

    a. Jeffords' Democrats
    b. Blue Dogs
    c. Kingdom Kings
    d. Red Cats

892. Vermont's primary election is held

    a. the first Tuesday in June.
    b. the second Tuesday in June.
    c. the first Tuesday in September.
    d. the second Tuesday in September.

893. Which of the following offices in Vermont was the last to be filled by a woman?

    a. Auditor of Accounts
    b. Treasurer
    c. Lieutenant Governor
    d. Secretary of State

894. Which candidate for president received the lowest percent of the vote in Vermont?

    a. Goldwater 1964
    b. McGovern 1972
    c. Mondale 1984
    d. Bush 1992

895. There were 49 municipalities reporting votes from the Northeast Kingdom in 2000. How many did Albert Gore carry?

    a. 0
    b. 7
    c. 15
    d. 25

896. The most Republican municipality in Vermont in the 2000 presidential election was

    a. Proctor.
    b. Lemington.
    c. Thetford.
    d. Hardwick.

897. What did Senator James Jeffords' father do for a living when Jim graduated from college?

    a. He was a conductor on the Rutland Railroad.
    b. He was a dairy farmer from Shrewsbury.
    c. He was a school teacher in Shrewsbury.
    d. He was the Chief Justice of the Vermont Supreme Court.

898. How far from the polling place must a candidate stand on Election Day?

    a. 10 feet
    b. 4 rods
    c. 50 feet
    d. no set distance is required

899. What year did Patrick Leahy first win election to the United States Senate from Vermont?

    a. 1968
    b. 1974
    c. 1980
    d. 1982

900. Who was the only incumbent Republican governor ever to lose a primary for reelection to the governorship?

Match the opponents:

Winners		*Losers*
901. _____ Dean 1992		a. Smith
902. _____ Sanders 1990		b. Sanders
903. _____ Kunin 1986		c. McClaughry
904. _____ Smith 1988		d. both Smith and Sanders

905. Howard Dean has never lost a statewide election in Vermont.

    a. True
    b. False

906. Against whom did Fred Tuttle run in the 1998 general election for the United States Senate?

a. John McClaughry
b. Jack McMullen
c. Pat Leahy
d. Bernard Sanders

907. Which of the following Vermont politicians did *not* write a book about their experiences?

a. Phil Hoff
b. Ralph Wright
c. Madeleine Kunin
d. George Aiken

908. Vermont's statewide percentage for Perot in 1992 was

a. 3.
b. 13.
c. 23.
d. 33.

Although political polls are common these days in Vermont, this was not always the case. Vermont's most famous pollster in the 1960s and early 1970s was Vincent (909.) _____ of (910.) _____ College , who discovered a "bellwether" town in Vermont named (911.) _____.

912. Pat Buchanan received less than one percent of the vote in Vermont in the presidential election of 2000.

a. True
b. False

913. Vermont now sends only one representative to Congress. But there was a time when Vermont sent

a. 3 representatives.
b. 6 representatives.
c. 9 representatives.

914. Ralph Nader got only seven percent of the vote in Vermont in the presidential election of 2000.

   a. True
   b. False

915. It is well known that in 1936 Vermont was one of two states to vote against Roosevelt and for Alfred M. Landon (81,023 to 62,124; the Communist candidate, Earl Browder, got 405 votes). There was one other presidential election in the 20th century in which Vermont was one of two states to vote for a loser. Which one was it?

Match the party with the politician:

916. _____ Fred Tuttle   a. Libertarian
917. _____ Matthew Mulligan   b. Liberty Union
918. _____ Hugh Douglas   c. Vermont Grassroots
919. _____ Peter Diamondstone   d. Republican

920. The Vermont Constitution says that each town "ought" to maintain a school. The Supreme Court says the Constitution really means "shall." The constitution also says all Christians "ought" to observe the Sabbath and worship God. Does this mean we can be fined for not going to church?

   a. yes
   b. no
   c. the Court doesn't say

921. What percent of the members of the Vermont Senate elected in 2000 were born in Vermont?

   a. 43%
   b. 53%
   c. 63%
   d. 73%

922. In 1958 he pulled off a remarkable upset in Vermont politics. He was the first and only Democrat to be elected to the U.S. House of Representatives from Vermont in the 20th century. Who was he?

923. How many electoral votes does Vermont have?

Match the percentage of the vote received with the presidential primary candidate:

924. _____ Jesse Jackson 1988	a.	44%
925. _____ Pat Buchanan 1996	b.	60%
926. _____ Bill Bradley 2000	c.	26%
927. _____ John McCain 2000	d.	17%

928. The county that gave the highest percentage of its votes to President Bush in 2000 was

    a. Orange.
    b. Rutland.
    c. Bennington.
    d. Essex.

Answers
A Modest Anarchism

876. b. Norwich.
877. b. 1916
878. c. a statewide referendum to allow localities to sell alcoholic beverages was passed.
879. d. 16
880. b. 1952
881. d. Peter Diamondstone
882. b. 1902.
883. b. The Brigham Decision.
884. c. Thomas Bahre—Addison
885. a. Nancy Chard—Windham
886. b. Vincent Illuzzi—Orleans
887. d. Richard McCormack—Windsor
888. c. Essex
889. F. Ray Keyser, Jr. Philip Hoff beat him in 1962.
890. c. a joint legislative assembly decides.
891. b. Blue Dogs
892. d. the second Tuesday in September.
893. a. Auditor of Accounts
894. d. Bush 1992
895. b. 7
896. b. Lemington, where Bush won 41 to 17.
897. d. Chief Justice of the Vermont Supreme Court
898. d. no set distance
899. b. 1974
900. Mortimer Proctor, in 1946.
901. c. McClaughry
902. a. Smith
903. d. both Smith and Sanders
904. b. Sanders
905. a. True

906. b. Jack McMullen
907. a. Phil Hoff. Aiken's is entitled *Speaking from Vermont*; Kunin's is entitled *Living a Political Life*; Wright's is entitled *All Politics is Personal*. Madeleine Kunin's book contains no table of contents or index. There is no way to determine what is in it or where any topic might be without reading it page by page. Still . . . it's well worth the effort.
908. c. 23, one of the highest in the nation.
909. Naramore
910. St. Michael's
911. Salisbury
912. a. True
913. b. 6.
914. a. True
915. In 1912 Vermont joined Utah to vote for Taft, who lost to Wilson.
916. d. Fred Tuttle—Republican
917. c. Matthew Mulligan—Vermont Grassroots
918. a. Hugh Douglas—Libertarian
919. b. Peter Diamondstone—Liberty Union
920. c. the Court doesn't say.
921. a. 43%
922. William H. Meyer
923. 3
924. c. Jesse Jackson—26%
925. d. Pat Buchanan—17%
926. a. Bill Bradley—44%
927. b. John McCain—60%
928. d. Essex was the only county to cast over half its votes for Bush (54%).

THE SPORTS PAGES

929. He is the first American born player to score 50 goals in three consecutive seasons in the National Hockey League. He hails from St. Albans. He is _____.

930. Many of the most sought-after basketball players in the history of the state were sisters like Jade (Vanderbilt) and Jazz (North Carolina) Huntington. For which high school did they play?

   a. Spaulding
   b. Burlington
   c. Brattleboro
   d. Oxbow

931. Another pair of sisters (Ashley and Morgan Valley) recruited by a powerhouse basketball program played for Rice High School. Both accepted athletic scholarships at

   a. Tennessee.
   b. Texas Tech.
   c. UVM.
   d. Connecticut.

Match the sport with the sportsperson:

_____ 932. Larry Benoit   a. kayak racing
_____ 933. Terry White   b. long-distance ice skating
_____ 934. Mike Armstrong   c. boxing
_____ 935. Bobby Dragon   d. deer hunting
_____ 936. Docke Dam   e. race car driving

937. What do *Devil's Bowl*, *Thunder Road*, and *Bear Ridge* all refer to?

On October 5, 1919, (938.) _____ (player), playing for the (939.) _____ (team), hit a home run playing against the Rutland baseball team.

182

940. In 1993, Patty Sheehan of Middlebury was inducted into the Hall of Fame for

a. golf.
b. table tennis.
c. bowling.
d. archery.

Match the name of the high school team with the high school:

_____ 941. Eagles	a. Otter Valley Union
_____ 942. Bobwhites	b. Brattleboro
_____ 943. Seahorses	c. Mt. Abraham
_____ 944. Colonels	d. St. Johnsbury
_____ 945. Hilltoppers	e. Burlington
_____ 946. Otters	f. BFA, St. Albans

947. Winner of national high school cross-country championships in 1997 and 1998, Erin Sullivan continues to star at Stanford. What Vermont high school did she attend?

a. South Burlington High School
b. Essex High School
c. Brattleboro High School
d. Mount Mansfield Union High School

Match these great coaches of the past with the sports they are best known for:

_____ 948. Ed Markey	a. schoolboy football
_____ 949. Mona Garone	b. basketball (college)
_____ 950. Denis E. Lambert	c. baseball
_____ 951. Ralph Lapointe	d. boxing
_____ 952. Dr. Donald Veburst	e. basketball (high school)

In the 1950s a basketball team from Vermont became a national contender. The team was known as the (953.) _____ Knights. They represented (954.) _____ College and were coached by (955.) _____.

956. In 1999 football star Nate Long of Burlington High School rushed over

   a. 1000 yards.
   b. 2000 yards.
   c. 3000 yards.
   d. 4000 yards.

957. Southeastern Vermont, especially Putney, has been the home of world-class athletes in this sport for years. They have put America on the map in a sport long dominated by Europeans. What is it?

958. One of America's best-known sportscasters and *the* most recognized in auto racing (because of his association with CBS) worked for years at WDEV, "The Voice of Vermont," in Waterbury. His name is _____ _____.

959. One of Vermont's best long-distance runners was Judi St. Hilaire, an All-American at UVM. St. Hilaire took 7th place at the 1991 World Track and Field Championships and came in 8th in the 10,000 meter finals in the Barcelona Olympics. She is a native of

   a. St. Johnsbury.
   b. Kirby.
   c. Lyndonville.
   d. Springfield.

960. Who is Vermont's best-ever baseball player? Hint: He played for the Red Sox and won two World Series.

961. During 1991–92 and 1992–93 the UVM Women's Basketball team

   a. had absolutely no player injuries.
   b. broke the record for points scored in a season.
   c. went undefeated.
   d. changed coaches 2 times.

Answers
The Sports Pages

929. John LeClair
930. d. Oxbow in Bradford
931. d. Connecticut.
932. d. Larry Benoit of Duxbury is to Vermont deer hunting what Ali was to boxing.
933. a. Terry White, a 1983 silver medallist in Holland, dominated U.S. kayak racing in the early 1980's.
934. c. Mike Armstrong—boxing
935. e. Bobby Dragon—race car driving
936. b. Docke Dam, a Panton dairy farmer, is a veteran long-distance skater who has competed in the longest races in the world. He once almost lost a finger when he fell and was run over by another skater.
937. Race tracks in West Haven, Barre, and Bradford
938. Babe Ruth
939. Boston Red Sox
940. a. golf (LPGA).
941. c. Mt. Abraham Eagles
942. f. BFA Bobwhites
943. e. Burlington Seahorses
944. b. Brattleboro Colonels
945. d. St. Johnsbury Hilltoppers
946. a. Otter Valley Otters
947. d. Mount Mansfield Union High School
948. b. Ed Markey—basketball (college)
949. e. Mona Garone—basketball (high school)
950. a. Denis E. Lambert—schoolboy football
951. c. Ralph Lapointe—baseball
952. d. Dr. Donald Veburst—boxing
953. Iron (Because the 5 starters played so much of each game. The team is commonly known as the "Purple Knights.")
954. St. Michael's
955. Doc Jacobs
956. c. 3,232 to be exact.

957. Nordic Skiing
958. Ken Squiers
959. c. Lyndonville
960. Larry Gardner
961. c. went undefeated

SCENES FIT FOR A POSTCARD

Most of Vermont is beautiful, but there are some places that are, simply, "pretty as a postcard." Identify the following vistas that draw the photographers year after year.

962.

963.

964.

Answers
Fit for a Postcard

962. East Corinth
963. Newbury
964. Strafford Meeting House